Believer's PREACHING Handbook

Andrew W. Wilson

Believer's Preaching Handbook: The Ten Elements of Excellent Preaching

Copyright © 2023 Andrew W. Wilson

Believers Publications, P. O. Box 485, North Lakes, Queensland, 4509, Australia

All rights reserved. No part of this publication may be reproduced or transmitted in any form or by any means, electronic or mechanical, including photocopy, recording or otherwise, except for brief quotations in printed reviews, without the written permission of the publisher.

Scripture quotations, unless otherwise noted, are taken from the New King James Version, copyright © 1979, 1980, 1982 by Thomas Nelson, Inc. Used by permission. All rights reserved.

Scripture quotations marked (KJV) are taken from The Holy Bible, Authorized King James Version

Scripture quotations marked (ESV) are taken from The Holy Bible, English Standard Version® (ESV®), copyright © 2001 by Crossway Bibles, a publishing ministry of Good News Publishers. Used by permission. All rights reserved.

Scripture quotations marked (NIV) are taken from the Holy Bible, New International Version®, NIV®, copyright © 1973, 1978, 1984, 2011 by Biblica, Inc.™ Used by permission of Zondervan. All rights reserved worldwide. www.zondervan.com The "NIV" and "New International Version" are registered in the United States Patent and Trademark Office by Biblica, Inc.™

ISBN: 978-0-9943977-4-4

CONTENTS

| | Acknowledgments and Abbreviations | 1 |

SECTION ONE: PREACHING

1	Why Preach?	4
2	The Seven Worst Sorts of Preaching	5
3	What is Good Preaching?	7

SECTION TWO: THE TEN ELEMENTS

4	Spiritual Power	12
5	Biblical Faithfulness	16
6	Doctrinal Substance	20
7	One Main Idea	21
8	Clear Structure	23
9	Introductions	28
10	Illustrations	30
11	Applications	32
12	Conclusions	34
13	Helpful Delivery	35

SECTION THREE: STUDYING THE BIBLE IN PREPARATION FOR PREACHING

14	Spiritual Principles of Preaching	38
15	Meditation	42
16	The Big Idea and Structure	45
17	The Sermon Summary Statement	47
18	Filling out the Sermon	49
19	Emphasis, Order and Context	50
20	Asking the Right Questions	52
21	Word Studies	54
22	Structure	56
23	Helps and Books	58
24	Sermon Preparation Timetable	60
25	Preparing for Delivering the Sermon	63

SECTION FOUR: PREACHING DIFFERENT TYPES OF SERMONS

26	Topical Preaching	68
27	Textual Preaching	70
28	Character Studies	72
29	Gospel Preaching	74
30	Preaching on Narratives	76
31	Preaching on Poetry	78
32	Small Group Studies	80
33	Youth Talks	82

SECTION FIVE: CHILDREN'S MESSAGES

34	Bible Storytelling	86
35	Preparing for Teaching Children	91
36	Increasing Your Impact	95
	Bibliography	100
	Other books by the Author	101

ACKNOWLEDGMENTS

This book has benefitted from interaction with, and feedback from, numerous students who have gone through the ACTS course over the last few years. The book is a compilation of the notes that were originally written for their benefit and refined in preaching training. In addition, this book would not have been written without the help of many other books on the subject of preaching. Just as I have never read a book on preaching without benefitting in some way from the wisdom of others, so too I hope that this book will encourage you to improve your preaching. Lastly, I want to thank God for His help in preaching the 'glorious gospel of the blessed God which was committed to my trust' (1 Timothy 1:11).

ABBREVIATIONS

cf.	compare with
Darby	J. N. Darby's New Translation
ESV	English Standard Version
Gk.	Greek
Heb.	Hebrew
KJV	King James Version
lit.	literally
LXX	Septuagint (Greek translation of the Hebrew Scriptures)
NIV	New International Version
NKJV	New King James Version
NT	New Testament
OT	Old Testament
RV	Revised Version

Preach the Word! Be ready in season and out of season.
Convince, rebuke, exhort with all longsuffering and doctrine
2 Timothy 4:2

SECTION ONE:

Preaching

1 WHY PREACH?

'Public speaking is listed as Americans' number 1 fear, before death at number 5, and loneliness weighing in at number 7. Guess that means that most of us are less afraid of dying alone than making a fool of ourselves in front of others' (Anne Cooper Ready, *Off the Cuff*, 2004, p19)

Here are three reasons why we should preach God's Word
1. It is God's command. 2 Timothy 4:2 says 'Preach the word! Be ready in season and out of season. Convince, rebuke, exhort, with all longsuffering and teaching'. Jesus said, 'Go into all the world and preach the gospel to every creature' (Mk. 16:15). In John Bunyan's day, the government forbad anyone preaching who was not ordained by the Church (and therefore approved by the government, for the church was controlled by the government). John Bunyan, the author of *Pilgrim's Progress*, preached anyway, and was thrown in prison. He defied the government and preached because it is God's command that His gospel should be preached. Today, we do not have any restrictions on preaching the Word of God, so we should be all the more active in doing so.
2. It is God's Word which saves and builds up. In Mark 4:14 Jesus explained the parable of the sower by saying 'The sower sows the word'. In Acts 20:32, Paul said, 'So now, brethren, I commend you to God and to the word of His grace, which is able to build you up and give you an inheritance among all those who are sanctified'. 'Nothing has won more souls or changed more lives or built up as many saints or strengthened more churches than faithful preaching' (Michael Raiter, Australian preacher).
3. People need to hear God's Word – whether they realise it or not. We need to do our best to make it really good! Philip Jensen (another Australian preacher) says: 'There are certain issues in ministry that you're going to be fighting about. Therefore, you mustn't fight over the ones you don't have to fight about. You've got to choose which hill you're going to be dying on. I think expounding the Scriptures is the hill to die on. So I wouldn't go for negotiation over that … [and that means that] when I actually do preach, I've got to be really good'.

John Wycliffe, the 'morning star of the Reformation' said that preaching is 'the highest service that man may attain to on earth'.

2. THE SEVEN WORST SORTS OF PREACHING

1. **The Wolf in Sheep's Clothing:** The worst sort of preaching is False Teaching (Acts 20:29-30).
2. **The Dump Truck:** A huge download of information, but not easy to listen to, digest, or follow.
3. **The Drone:** Boring and monotonous. Mark Twain said about one preacher that 'he more than made up in length what he lacked in depth'. My grandfather used to describe some preachers as having 'buckets of words, thimbles of thoughts'.
4. **The Rambler:** No Structure to the Message, wandering all over the place. Some preachers are like Christopher Columbus: when he started out he didn't know where he was going, when he got there he didn't know where he was, and when he got back no one knew where he had been.
5. **The Clown:** In the 1980s Neil Postman wrote a secular book called, *Amusing Ourselves to Death*. The great preacher Spurgeon said: 'the time will come when instead of shepherds feeding the sheep, the church will have clowns entertaining goats'.
6. **The Drowning Man:** here is someone out of depth in the Bible passage. We need to be very familiar with God's Word to preach on it. This means that we need to be reading through the entire Bible (or at least the New Testament) every year. A variant on this sort of preacher is the Swimmer with Floaties. This is the preacher who is so out of his depth in a passage that he does not try to dive in. Instead of digging into the passage, he just gives a very shallow and superficial message with no real insights.
7. **The Coach:** there are some churches where people are told, 'you don't need to bring a Bible'. Instead of preaching from God's Word, all that the congregation gets is "motivational talks" (based on a dream, or 'prophecy') which are used to challenge and encourage people to get more involved in the great work that God is doing through the church through giving more money and getting involved in serving. Or, the messages will be a mixture of a self-help seminar and a stand-up comedy act – all intended to help you live 'your best life now'.

Twelve Bad Habits in Preaching

- Preaching based on an initial impression we get from a passage instead of a deep understanding of its message: Matthew Henry wrote: 'Study close; especially make the Bible your study. There is no knowledge, which I am more desirous to increase in, than that. Men get wisdom by books; but wisdom towards God is to be gotten out of God's book; and that by digging. Most men do but walk over the surface of it, and pick up here and there a flower. Few dig into it' (Charles Bridges, *The Christian Ministry*, 1849, p51, note 1).
- Preaching which consists of little disconnected sermonettes unrelated to a central theme
- Preaching which links together a number of related Scriptures (concordance sermons)
- Preaching which consists of running comments or a rambling collection of disjointed thoughts on the verses in a passage (this is commenting, not preaching; no structure).
- Preaching which presents a download of information with no application for listener's lives (grammatical analysis of Greek words, quotes from commentaries, history of Roman emperors, etc.).
- Preaching in which we read our own eccentric convictions into a text instead of letting the text shape our doctrine (this is imposition, not exposition – John Stott)
- Preaching which majors on minor points and ignores the main message of a passage
- Preaching with no real understanding of the passage, based on a superficial and shallow study of it
- Preaching which labours the obvious and avoids the difficult
- Preaching which refers to endless Bible verses ('a paper trail')
- Preaching based on an illustration rather than the main point of the passage
- Preaching based on an application from the passage instead of the main point of the passage

3 WHAT IS GOOD PREACHING?

SEVEN DEFINITIONS OF PREACHING

1. A Biblical Definition

Haggai 1:13 – 'Haggai the LORD's messenger spoke the LORD's message to the people'.

- Preaching is the delivery of a message from God through His servant

2. A Good Definition of Preaching

Preaching is 'getting the truth of God out of the Bible and getting it across to other people'.

3. D. Martyn Lloyd-Jones (*Preaching and Preachers*)

'Preaching is Logic on Fire'. This definition lacks some important elements, particularly God's Word

4. Phillip Brooks (*Lectures on Preaching*, p8)

'Truth poured through personality'. This definition is helpful in highlighting the personal element in preaching.

5. Jay Adams (*Pulpit Speech*, p 6)

Preaching involves four arts: (1) Researching Content, (2) The Art of Organisation, (3) The Art of Language usage, (4) The Art of Delivery. This definition leaves me stone COLD, because it reduces preaching to a merely mechanical manipulation of words. It leaves out the divine, spiritual element.

6. A. T. Pierson

'A sermon is a discourse on Scripture that is designed to save or edify the hearer'. The strength of this definition is that is reminds us that preaching is intended to achieve some end. Preaching must be more than simply the delivery of information.

7. Haddon W. Robinson (*Biblical Preaching*, p21)

'Expository preaching is the communication of a biblical concept, derived from and transmitted through a historical, grammatical, and literary study of a passage in its context, which the Holy Spirit first applies to the personality and experience of the preacher, then through the preacher, applies to the hearers'. This definition is a bit too wordy and congested, but it contains lots of truth.

Robinson's four key components in this definition:
(a) A Biblical Concept
(b) Based on the study of a Passage of Scripture in its Setting,
(c) Experienced in the Preacher's own life by the power of the Spirit
(d) Communicated and applied to the hearers

OVERVIEW OF THE TEN ELEMENTS OF EXCELLENT PREACHING
In this book, we are going to primarily focus on expository preaching. E. M. Bounds said this about expository preaching:

> Topical preaching, polemical preaching, historical preaching, and other forms of sermonic output have, one supposes, their rightful and opportune uses. But expository preaching – the prayerful expounding of the Word of God – is preaching that is preaching, pulpit effort *par excellence*.

We are going to focus on ten features of good preaching. Here they are:
1. **Spiritual Power** – God's help, presence and blessing
2. **Biblical Faithfulness** – It Accurately Preaches the Word and Explains the Bible Correctly
3. **One Main Idea** – Every Sermon should have just One Big Theme
4. **Clear Structure** – Not Difficult to Follow
5. **Doctrinal Substance** – Not Majoring on Minors, riding hobby-horses
6. **Inviting Introduction** – Arousing Interest in the Message
7. **Vivid Illustration** – Holding Attention and Explaining Difficulties
8. **Practical Application** – Pricking Consciences and Changing Lives
9. **Helpful Delivery** – a Speaker's Words and Actions should not Detract from the Message

10. **Challenging Conclusion** - A Good Ending

Wow – that's a lot to get right, if our preaching is going to be good! Preaching is hard work. W. E. Sangster said: 'Preaching will require more than a few thoughts that come to a man while he is waiting in a bus queue'. How do we get better at it? By doing it. The English preacher G. H. Lang said, 'The way to do it is to do it'.

Which of these ten elements of preaching are the most important? This is somewhat subjective, but in my opinion, the top two features of preaching are biblical faithfulness and spiritual power. If someone is preaching something that is not faithful to God's Word, then this is the worst sort of preaching. But God's Spirit's help and power is so essential to biblical preaching that without it, our preaching is nothing.

Biblical faithfulness also requires that the preacher goes down through the passage bringing out important truths from it, not just presenting a sermon title, an alliterative outline, and then skating over the passage itself. Putting some 'flesh on the bones', that is, unpacking insights into what each verse is saying, is more important than having 'One Main Idea' or a 'Clear Structure'. However, without 'One Main Idea' and 'Clear Structure', the message will be more difficult for listeners to follow. Some preaching consists of 'three points', but the three points are not connected in any way to each other or the Main Idea – they are just three mini-sermonettes. Therefore, identifying the One Main Idea of a passage is more important than having a nice alliterative outline. The best preaching, however, has both One Main Idea and a Clear Structure that connects to, and divides up, the Main Idea.

Some preaching fails because it does not have any application or illustration, but it is even worse if the sermon is all application and illustration without faithful, in-depth biblical exposition. Having a nice introduction is no use unless it leads into powerful presentation of God's truth. Thus, the first five elements (Spiritual Power, Biblical Faithfulness, One Main Idea, Clear Structure and Doctrinal Substance) are more important than the second five elements (Introduction, Illustration,

Application, Conclusion and Helpful Delivery).

Someone has said, 'A good sermon stretches the mind, tans the hide, warms the heart and provokes the will'.

Section Two:

The Ten Elements of Excellent Preaching

4 SPIRITUAL POWER
God's help, Presence and Blessing in Preaching

Why is some preaching arresting and powerful, but some boring or flat? The answer is that all true preaching must be based upon a living relationship with God, prayerful seeking for God's help in preparation, and God's power experienced in delivery. All preaching without the Spirit's power, however gifted the preacher or technically perfect the sermon, is just a talk – a performance, a 'show'.

In Luke's Gospel we read about the beginning of our Lord's ministry: 'Then Jesus returned in the power of the Spirit to Galilee, and news of Him went out through all the surrounding region. And He taught in their synagogues, being glorified by all' (Luke 4:14-15).

The apostle Paul similarly wrote, 'For our gospel did not come to you in word only, but also in power, and in the Holy Spirit and in much assurance (1 Thess. 1:5). In 1 Cor. 2:4, he wrote, 'my speech and my preaching were not with persuasive words of human wisdom, but in demonstration of the Spirit and of power'.

The most essential feature of great preaching is Spiritual Power. This does not mean preaching about any ideas that come into our heads in the Spirit's power. We must preach the Word of God for, as John Knox the Scottish Reformer said to Queen Mary, 'the Spirit in the Word is never contrarious to Himself'. Sometimes people today say that the Spirit of God has told them some idea, but if we can't find it in the Word of God, we can be sure it is not from the Spirit of God at all. Therefore, Spiritual Power is also crucial to Biblical Faithfulness.

Some Quotes about Spiritual Power in Preaching
- 'In the name of God, brethren, labour to awaken your own hearts, before you go to the pulpit, that you may be fit to awaken the hearts of sinners' (Richard Baxter).
- 'The great want of today is a holier ministry ... we need men of God

who bring the atmosphere of heaven with them to the pulpit and speak from the borders of another world' (Anonymous)
- Preaching is logic on fire (M. Lloyd-Jones)
- 'You will find that the learned authorities often, if not generally, disagree with one another completely, and the meaning ultimately has to be determined not by some exact science but by spiritual perception, spiritual understanding, that 'unction' that John talks about in 1 John 2:20, 27 (Lloyd-Jones).
- 'The best preaching in the world without the Spirit's touch, is nothing' (Stuart Olyott).
- There is an old saying: 'Study yourself full, write yourself clear, pray yourself hot, and preach yourself empty'.
- [We should preach] As one that ne'er should preach again, And as a dying man to dying men (Baxter).
- William McDonald: 'A man may be highly talented, very well trained, and widely experienced… but without spiritual power he is ineffective. On the other hand… a man may be uneducated, unattractive, and unrefined… yet let him be endued with the power of the Holy Spirit and people will turn out to see him burn for God'.

I once listened to a brother preaching about his ministry of evangelistic door-knocking. Although he was no doubt a good talker on the door-step, he was no good in the pulpit. A friend of mine who was listening to him was so disappointed that picked up his Bible and started reading it. I asked him later what he thought of the man, and his two-word reply was, 'No Fire'.

In what elements of preaching do we need the help of the Holy Spirit?
- In finding the 'central truth' of a passage,
- in understanding difficult verses,
- in setting out a clear structure for our message,
- in finding good illustrations and applications,
- we need to be filled with the Spirit in our preaching,
- we need Him to work by convicting hearts of hearers, in convincing

of sin, in converting and transforming lives.

HOW DO WE OBTAIN THE SPIRIT'S POWER IN PREACHING?

1. We need to ask for it. (Luke 11:13). George Whitefield silently prayed as he entered the pulpit: Assist my by Thy grace!
2. The preacher must drop from his life everything that grieves the Spirit (Eph. 4:30)
3. We must 'give ourselves continually to prayer and the ministry of the word' (Acts 6:4), so that we are full of the Word of God, full of Christ, full of the Holy Spirit (Eph. 5:18, Col. 3:16)
4. We must preach Christ – make Him the centre of our message – the Spirit loves to glorify Christ (John 16:14). It is 'Christ lifted up' that draws people to the Savior (John 12:32)
5. E. M. Bounds: 'How and whence comes this unction [i.e. anointing, spiritual power]? Direct from God in answer to prayer. Praying hearts only are the hearts filled with this holy oil; praying lips only are anointed with this divine unction. Prayer, much prayer, is the price of preaching unction; prayer, much, prayer, is the one, sole condition of keeping this unction. Without unceasing prayer the unction never comes to the preacher. Without perseverance in prayer, the unction, like the manna overkept, breeds worms'.
6. 'Power with God and man' (Gen. 32:24-7) comes from wrestling with God like Jacob did, not letting go until He has blessed us.

E. M. Bounds wrote, 'It is not great talents nor great learning nor great preaching that God needs, but men great in holiness, great in faith, great in love, great in fidelity, great for God – men always preaching by holy sermons in the pulpit, but holy lives out of it'.

George Muller wrote, 'I saw more clearly than ever, that the first great and primary business to which I ought to attend every day was to have my soul happy in the Lord. The first thing to be concerned about was not how much I might serve the Lord, or how I might glorify the Lord; but how I might get my soul into a happy state, and how my inner man might be nourished'. The most important part of a preacher's life is his daily communion with God. If we spend much time here, we will experience much help in serving God. Our daily walk with God is the source of our spiritual power.

Henry Craik, George Muller's co-worker, said this: 'They who would seek in modern days to carry on, in any measure, the cause to which the Apostles were devoted, must cultivate an habitual sense of dependence leading to persevering prayer. They must, above things, honour the Divine Spirit, and trust to His effectual agency for the success of their labours. No knowledge, even of Scripture, no natural capabilities, no acquired attainments, must be allowed to supersede the necessity of constant waiting upon God for the supply of power from on High. The training of a university, or the humbler aid of a [Bible] college, will be found miserable substitutes for the teaching of the Spirit, and the energy of His inward operations. Discourses may be prepared with assiduous care, and delivered with propriety and animation; crowds of interested listeners may be attracted by the natural endowments of the preacher, and yet he may be unto his hearers -" as a very lovely song of one that hath a pleasant voice, and can play well on an instrument, for they hear his words but they do them not"'.

I once heard a preacher tell a story about how he had prepared one of the best messages he had ever preached, and it was still only Tuesday in the week before he had to preach it. He was looking forward to preaching this great message on the weekend. But instead of spending the rest of the week praying for the Lord's help in preaching, he sat back and enjoyed thinking about how good it was going to be. Sadly, when Sunday came, his message was a flop.

5 BIBLICAL FAITHFULNESS
IT ACCURATELY PREACHES THE WORD AND EXPLAINS THE BIBLE CORRECTLY

All true preaching must be based upon God's Word. If our preaching is not based on God's Word, it has no real authority – it is merely our ideas, our opinions, or our sentimental moralising. No one wants to hear us on these topics – they want to hear from God.

Donald Miller: 'Every sermon should have a theme, and that theme should be the theme of the portion of Scripture on which it is based'.

Haddon Robinson: 'In many sermons the biblical passage ... resembles the national anthem played at a baseball game – it gets things started but is not heard again'.

One of my sons had a Religious Instruction lesson in a state school where the story was about King Hezekiah and the Assyrian emperor Sennacharib. This is a story with great lessons about faith in God and salvation. But the teacher (a Christian) either did not know what to say about this story, or preferred to talk about something more exciting, so after five minutes about Hezekiah, she held up a picture. The children were told that it was a painting of Jesus drawn by a young girl. The reason we know that this is what Jesus looks like, the class were told, was because of a young boy who died and claimed he went to heaven and came back (and a book was written about what he saw in heaven). This boy was shown the painting and he said that this was what Jesus looked like.

Leaving aside questions of whether we should believe this story or not, and the additional fact that what the teacher did was illegal (in the state where we lived, teachers were required to stick to the curriculum), the point here is that this teacher's message was not faithful to the Bible story she was supposed to tell.

Our preaching should be based upon God's Word, the Bible. Liberal theologians prefer to preach on some headline they have seen in the newspaper, and some people prefer to preach on their dreams. But we should preach what God has said in His word. Jeremiah attacked the false-prophets of his day with these words: 'The prophet who has a dream, let him tell a dream; And he who has My word, let him speak My word faithfully. What is the chaff to the wheat?' says the LORD. 'Is not My word like a fire?' says the LORD, 'And like a hammer that breaks the rock in pieces?' (Jer. 23:28-29).

Biblical faithfulness requires that we be able to show that the points we make in our message are derived from the Bible. Unless we can back up each point from Scripture, and show listeners where we get it, we are not representing God, nor will we convince listeners to change their lives to follow God's will.

Martyn Lloyd-Jones said this about the preparation of the sermon: 'Well, obviously the first thing you have to do is to deal with the meaning of your text. At this point there is one golden rule ... honesty. You have to be honest with your text ... you do not go to a text just to pick out an idea which interests you and then deal with that idea yourself ... you must take your text in its context... you must discover the meaning of the words and of the whole statement' (*Preaching and Preachers*, pp199, 201).

One of the biggest problems in modern-day preaching is people being asked to speak on passages they are not very familiar with. We need to read the entire Bible regularly, and study its books – so we have our own messages to preach from the Lord. When asked to speak on an unfamiliar passage, we need to read it many times prayerfully, in different versions, asking God's help to become familiar with it and understand its true message.

HOW DO WE GET GOD'S TRUTH OUT OF GOD'S WORD?
We need to prayerfully meditate on it. What does this mean?
- Read the passage,
- jot down notes,
- summarise it,
- paraphrase it,
- look for key words.
- R. T. Kendall said: 'I'm looking for insights'

HOW DO WE ENSURE OUR PREACHING IS BIBLICALLY FAITHFUL?

- Familiarity with the passage is the most important way to be biblically faithful in our preaching
- Read the entire Bible (or at least the NT) regularly (e.g. yearly), so it is not unfamiliar material to us.
- By studying the Bible passage diligently and carefully in preparation
- By understanding the words the Bible passage uses to convey its truth.
- By interpreting the Bible passage correctly, that is, by carefully considering the context of our passage to make sure we have not mistaken the meaning, and by considering other Bible cross-references that help to explain what our passage might mean (Scripture is its own interpreter).
- By reading out the passage at the start of our message when we preach on it
- By 'grounding' the points we make in our preaching, that is, referring to the verse our point comes from, and not just pointing out the verse number, but reading out the very words that prove our point.

DANGERS IN PREACHING

- If our preaching is not based on God's Word, it has no real authority – it is merely our ideas, our opinions on current affairs or political questions, or our sentimental moralising. Who wants to hear that?
- We must not read our own ideas or doctrinal opinions into a passage (Stott: this is imposition, not exposition). For example, one man in my youth was always preaching against charismatics. In a sermon on Judas, he would start preaching against the prosperity Gospel and Christian preachers appealing for money. Instead, we must let the passage shape our message.
- Ripping things out of context. For example, Muslims take John 14:16, where Jesus prayed the Father to give the disciples another Helper, to refer to Muhammed. But the rest of this verse disproves this idea: Jesus said that this comforter would abide with them forever.
- No insights into God's Word. My grandfather used to speak of some preachers who had ' buckets of words, but thimbles of thoughts'. I have heard other preachers described as 'labouring the obvious and avoiding the difficult'.

- The danger of trying to share all the results of our study in the sermon. I like to call this the 'iceberg' principle: a lot of our study preparation is best kept out of our sermon, just like the majority of an iceberg is under the water and not seen.

6 DOCTRINAL SUBSTANCE
Not Majoring on Minors

Sermons should increase our understanding of the big topics of the Bible: God, Sin, Salvation, Christ, Grace, Faith, Repentance, Sanctification, the Holy Spirit, Judgement, etc.

Martyn Lloyd-Jones wrote, 'What is the chief end of preaching? I like to think it is this. It is to give men and women a sense of God and His presence … some dim glimpse of the majesty and glory of God, the love of Christ my Saviour and the magnificence of the gospel'.

We want our listeners to go away with a greater view of God, so that as a result of the message they worship Him. We want to preach so that the gospel is clearly explained, so that listeners feel the sinfulness of sin, marvel at Christ giving himself for us, are filled with wonder at salvation by grace through faith, and hear the call to repentance.

The Irish preacher Willie Mullan said: 'your message is a failure if you don't get to the Cross'.

When we are preaching to Christians, we want to preach sermons so that believers are comforted by the blessings they have received, not confused about how Christians should live. We want to preach so that Christians' lives are transformed so that they are sitting at the Lord's feet, day by day, their prayer lives are not shallow but full, and their witness for Christ to others is clear.

We should not impose our doctrinal convictions on a passage, but rather bring out the doctrinal truth found in a passage. We should not major on minor points in a passage, but get to the heart of a passage. We should not preach messages which give a lop-sided and unbalanced explanation of a particular truth by focusing on certain verses in the Bible in a way that denies what other verses teach.

7 ONE MAIN IDEA
Every Sermon should have just One Major Theme

I have a friend who has a painting in his house. It is abstract art and the painting is composed of many different coloured paint spots on a white canvas. I don't think it is trying to convey any message or picture or point. Our preaching should not be like this! Nor should our preaching by trying to have many different points. It should focus our eyes on a central truth or message.

Donald Miller: 'Any single sermon should have just one major idea. The points or subdivisions should be parts of this one grand thought'.

Lloyd-Jones: 'What I am leading to ... is that you make certain that you are really getting the main message, the main thrust and import of this particular text or statement'.

Haddon Robinson: 'Ideally each sermon is the explanation, interpretation, or application of a single dominant idea supported by other ideas, all drawn from one passage or several passages' ... [In some sermons] listeners enjoy some human interest stories, jot down a catchy phrase and judge the sermon a success if it finishes on time. Important matters, like subject, escape them entirely ... Judging from the uncomprehending way in which listeners talk about a sermon, it is hard to believe that they have listened to a message. Instead, the responses indicate that they leave with a basketful of fragments but no adequate sense of the whole ... A sermon should be a bullet, not buckshot' (*Biblical Preaching*, 34-5).

Why Should a Sermon Have One Main Idea?

If a sermon has one main idea, it will have simplicity and a clear focus. There was a book written once with the title: You've got a point there. If our preaching had one main idea, people will see what out point is. If the main point of our sermon corresponds to the main point of the passage, people will clearly understand what God's Word is teaching. If our message draws together the various thoughts in a passage and presents the one main idea from them, it will show that Scripture is coherent and logical.

I once overheard a group of Christian ladies talking together. One of them reported to the others about how wonderful her preacher was on Sunday. But when she was asked by a friend what the preacher spoke about, there was only silence. The lady was not able to say. Every preacher should be so simple, clear and focused that everybody goes away knowing what he has spoken about.

How to Determine the Main Idea

Immerse yourself in a text until you have a clear idea what it is about!
- Prayerfully read the text, repeatly, in context
- Paraphrase the passage; write it in your words
- Try to understand who it was written to, and what issues they had
- Ask why the author has written it
- Highlight repeated words or themes
- Summarise its message

8 CLEAR STRUCTURE
NOT DIFFICULT TO FOLLOW

A Bible message should be like an arrow with three or four feathers to keep it on track. It should not be like a cow grazing, wandering from here to there. It was said of one preacher, that he was like Christopher Columbus, in that when he set out, he didn't know where he was going, when he got there he didn't know where he was, and when he got back nobody knew where he had been. This is not how we should preach.

Broadus: 'Let us carefully observe, then, that an expository sermon may have and must have both unity and an orderly structure ... If pressed for time, do not plan to read a passage of Scripture and make a few remarks. Such is not an expository sermon'.

WHAT DO WE MEAN BY CLEAR STRUCTURE?
We mean that our message uses Headings, or Divisions, or Points - firstly, secondly, thirdly ....
- G. Campbell-Morgan: The three essentials for great preaching are truth, clarity and passion.
- Cicero, the great Roman orator and statesman said that public speaking required three things: apte (i.e. appropriate content) distincte (clear message), ornate (beautiful words).

ADVANTAGES OF A CLEAR STRUCTURE:
- keeps the message focused,
- allows the listeners to follow what you're saying,
- is remembered for longer,
- breaks the message into smaller units,
- allows listeners to rejoin if their mind wanders, and
- allows you to speak from memory.

Spurgeon compared a sermon with no structure to the day as a boy he was sent to the shop with a basket to buy some rice, tea and mustard, but on the way home he chased a pack of hounds over hedge and ditch until when he reached home he found all the goods mixed together into one awful mess: 'I ... understood the necessity of packing up my subjects in good stout parcels ... and this makes me keep to firstly, secondly, and thirdly, however unfashionable that may now be. People will not drink your mustardy tea, nor will they enjoy muddled-up sermons, in which you cannot tell head and tail'.

Lloyd-Jones: 'Divide the teaching that you want to put to the people up into propositions or headings ... As far as I am concerned, if my sermon is not clear and ordered in my mind I cannot preach it to others. I suppose I could stand up and talk, but that would probably muddle people rather than help them. That is why I regard this ordering and shaping of the sermon as most important, and I advocate that you should struggle with this until you get it into shape'.

A. P. Gibbs said that if we do not have a clear structure, 'The danger in expository preaching is that it can become a collection of disconnected sermonettes'. Even worse is when a preacher makes a series of rambling remarks: "commenting". But nobody reads a commentary for pleasure, neither will listeners enjoy us if we preach like one.

How to Work out a Structure:
- Notice any divisions in a passage,
- Notice logical connections or contrasts between ideas, or progressions of thought
- Summarise these divisions/sections to get your headings, i.e. your sermon structure.

Different Types of Sermon

Expository sermons (dealing with a passage).
A. P. Gibbs lists seven benefits and one danger:
1. It puts supreme emphasis on the Word of God
2. It makes for a broad knowledge of the Scriptures
3. It provides opportunity for speaking on many passages otherwise neglected
4. It makes for variety in the ministry of the Word
5. It enables the preacher to deal with current evils without personal attacks
6. It delivers the preacher from the fanciful use or abuse of isolated texts
7. It will furnish the preacher with enough material for a lifetime of preaching
8. The DANGER: it can become a collection of disconnected sermonettes ('commenting')

Topical sermons (looking at a subject).
Its benefits are that it allows the great subjects of the Bible (both doctrinal or practical) to be dealt with, and it shows the unity of the Bible, as material is drawn from different passages throughout Scripture. The disadvantages are the limited number of main topics the Bible deals with and that listeners do not learn to read the Bible as given, i.e. in books.

Textual sermons (based on one verse).
Its benefit is that it explores in more depth the message of one verse. Because it is a short text, its message is more easily retained by an audience. The danger here is that the Bible is thought of as a book of isolated texts without any unity.

DIFFERENT TYPES OF SERMON OUTLINES

Natural Divisions. The best and clearest outlines, divisions, or structures for a sermon come straight from the Bible itself. Look for natural paragraph divisions in a passage, or key words in a verse.

Parallel Points. After identifying the main theme of a passage, we look to see what a passage says about this 'Big Idea'. Often there will be a number of things we learn about it. Look for Plural Abstract Nouns (e.g. lessons, benefits, blessings, requirements). Thus a message about Ephesians 2:1-10 might be Three Truths about Salvation. In 1 Thess. 1:1-10, we have Ten Evidences of Conversion. Advantages of this form of outline: it is easy to follow, and to reinforce the main idea repetitively.

Pearls on a string: Sometimes a passage has many things to say about one issue, e.g. James 3.

Sequential Story. Many Bible passages involve narratives, or a story that moves to a conclusion. Thus, a good structure will often trace the flow of the narrative: Problem, Solution, Application. Eph. 2:1-10 has three paragraphs about salvation: (1) Our Need, (2) God's Provision, (3) Our Acceptance. The Parable of the Prodigal Son has a number of movements: Rebellion, Ruin, Repentance, Reception. The disadvantage of a Sequential Story outline is that it can easily become a long ramble without structure, so that listeners get lost and tune out.

Question and Answer. Many topical sermons are best handled by asking questions – what, why, how, who, when, where? E.g. What is New Birth?

Why do we need it? How are we born again?

THE RULE OF THREE

What is the best number of main points in a message? There is no rule on the matter, other than trying to allow the Bible passage itself to determine the structure, if possible. Try to have variety in your outlines, so you do not become repetitive. But three points is always very easy to listen to (more than four points becomes hard for listeners to remember, while less than three points seems under-prepared). Christ often told parables that had three characters (the priest, levite and Samaritan, or three servants in the parable of the talents), or three parts (lost sheep, lost coin, lost son).

Even nursery rhymes often come in threes: the three little pigs, Goldilocks and three bears, Red Riding Hood (what big eyes you have, ears, teeth). Many jokes have three parts (Englishman, Scotsman, Irishman), as do many sayings ('I came, I saw, I conquered', Hear no evil, see no evil, speak no evil, On your mark, get set, go, The Good, the Bad, and the Ugly).

The famous preacher Alexander McLaren was said to be able to tap each passage with his 'golden hammer' and it would yield a perfect three-point sermon. For example, his sermon on Colossians 1:15-23 consisted of three points:
1. Christ's relation to God
2. Christ's relation to Creation
3. Christ's relation to the Church

TRANSITIONS

We also need to try and provide transitions from one main point of our message to the next.

Haddon Robinson: 'You must help your listeners separate your main points from the material that supports them. That's why it takes at least three or four statements and restatements of a point to make a point clear to an audience. Carefully constructed transitions help your listeners to think with you so that together you and they move through the sermon'.

Bryan Chappell lists suggests some different Types of Transitions, including:
- 'Knitting statements' (i.e. tying a previous point to the next one)– e.g. 'Not only ... but also', 'Next ...'

- 'Dialogical questions' (thinking out loud) – e.g. 'If this won't work, what will?', 'What comes next?'
- Numbering and listing: first, second, third .... WARNING: this is a dry and boring method

9 INTRODUCTIONS
HELPING PEOPLE TO START LISTENING

We want to arouse interest in the message, and get people to tune in to God's Word, to forget their own issues. Researchers say that you have about 30 seconds to convince your audience to listen to you. 'An introduction should present listeners with an arresting thought that draws them away from apathy or competing interests and makes them say, "Hey! I need to hear this!"'.

In Acts 17:3 we read that Paul in his preaching was 'opening and alleging' (KJV). He made an opening statement that drew people's attention to his message.

- 'Early in the sermon therefore, your listeners should realise that you are talking to them about themselves. You should raise a question, probe a problem, identify a need, open up a vital issue to which the passage speaks' (Haddon Robinson).
- One Preacher's Sermon Method: Connect , Explain , Reflect

HOW TO INTRODUCE A MESSAGE: USE A HOOK

We need to grab people's attention in our introduction. Some people describe this as using a 'hook', in the same way that we catch a fish on a line using a hook.

- You can tell a story to connect: 'Last October …'. People tune in to stories; they like to hear the ending..
- Give a startling statistic or factoid,
- Make a bold statement, or state a paradox
- You can raise a question that matters to the audience, or a problem needing solving.
- You can give two people's opinions about some matter, the ask: which is right?
- For children, you can even use an object lesson – that is, some visual picture or physical object that holds their attention and opens up the subject.

What Should you NOT do in an Introduction?

- Check the microphone is working, and ask how much time you have to speak – these things should all have been done before you start.
- Tell people your name, where you come from, and the subject of your talk – again, these should all be known by audience already, so there is no need to do this
- Spend the first half of your message going back over where you've been in a previous message.
- The Mystery Tour: a cryptic roundabout journey through apparently random passages from all over the Bible without telling anybody why you are reading these verses, only to tie it all together later into a point.
- Go on for too long with your introduction – it is meant to introduce the message, not be the message
- Tell a random joke to gain attention.

10 ILLUSTRATIONS
Holding Attention and Explaining Difficulties

If preaching is 'the fine art of speaking in someone else's sleep' (Chuck Swindoll), then we need to use the odd illustration to wake them up! The Lord used about fifty illustrations in the Sermon on the Mount. Between 50% and 75% of the Lord's teaching involved parables. He also used illustrations from nature (e.g. the birds of the air in Matt. 6:26).

- Abraham Lincoln said, "They say I tell a great many stories. I reckon I do, but I have found in the course of a long experience that common people, take them as they run, are more easily informed through the medium of a broad illustration than in any other way, and as to what the hyper-critical few may think, I don't care'.
- 'The amount of time that the average public assembly can listen to a sustained argument is strictly limited. Unless a man has before him a company of highly trained minds, he can only subject them to flinty thinking for short periods. They must rest mentally for a moment or two before moving on again' (W. E. Sangster, *The Craft of Sermon Illustration*).
- 'Be sure you do not go too long into the sermon without the break that a good helpful illustration affords, both to enlighten your point and to relieve the minds of those who are trying to follow your logic' (G. D. Fee, *New Testament Exegesis*).
- If you would attain simplicity in preaching, you must use plenty of anecdotes and illustrations (Ryle, *Simplicity in Preaching*)

What Illustrations Achieve
- Illustrations gain Interest and hold Attention,
- Illustrations give listeners a Rest,
- Illustrations Explain and Clarify truths using familiar language,
- Illustrations are Memorable – they plant your idea deep in your listeners' minds,
- Illustrations Convict, Persuade and Motivate,

- Illustrations allow you to repeatedly drive home your point, not only telling them the truth, but illustrating it, and then applying it.

What are some Dangers with Illustrations?

One danger is in using illustrations that glorify yourself. If you must speak of yourself in an illustration, it is best to use an illustration that shows your failures and weakness.

Sources of Illustrations

- Personal experience,
- imagination ("Imagine/Suppose there was a man ..."),
- fictional stories from popular culture – novels, movies, etc,
- current affairs, news items,
- historical facts,
- quotes from Christian writers, hymns, etc.,
- Christian biography,
- Bible stories

11 APPLICATIONS
PRICKING CONSCIENCES AND CHANGING LIVES

A preacher's task is not to deliver information, but to deliver a proclamation. You do not have a message until you have an application. Ask yourself what the relevance of this passage is for the listeners. What should listeners do today as a result? Different audiences will mean that we apply a passage in different ways; e.g. are we preaching to Christians or non-Christians, children or adults, 'humble or haughty' people? We might need to comfort the afflicted or afflict the comfortable.

- Sangster tells the story of a student at Bible college who had to preach a sermon to his class and then afterwards go and talk to the principal about it. He went to the principal and asked, 'It will do, won't it, sir?' The principal replied, 'Do what?'
- 'May the Holy Ghost apply this truth to our lives', says the preacher who does not have a ghost of a guess as to how the biblical content might change people' (Robinson).
- 'A sermon is a discourse on Scripture that is designed to save or edify the hearer' (A. T. Pierson). In other words, a sermon is intended to DO something. 'Preach for a verdict'. There are no theological exams in heaven; we must get people to act on biblical truth and faith.
- Abraham Lincoln (about a sermon): 'It was brilliantly conceived, biblical, relevant and well-presented'. Friend: 'so, it was a great sermon?' Lincoln: 'No. It failed. It failed because Dr. G. did not ask us to do something great'.
- F. B. Meyer: 'the Word of God was not given to be admired for its beauty or studied for its detail; it is given to be obeyed'.

Get Specific! Get Practical!
Give people something concrete to do on Monday in response to your message
- John the Baptist didn't just tell people to repent; he told them how to repent. In Luke 3:10-14, he gave specific, practical instructions to the people generally, to the tax-gatherers and to the soldiers.

- Think of the life situations of people in your audience and try to spell out what it would mean in practical terms for them to live out the Scripture. Use illustrations here again to give examples of how other people have obeyed the particular principle you are preaching about.
- Think of different people in your congregation (a mother, a teenager) and think of illustrations that will connect with these different groups (not just illustrations for yourself).
- It will always be easier for you to provide specific, practical applications if you yourself have tried to obey and put into practice the principle you are preaching about!

A Warning:
A text has one valid Interpretation (the author's intended meaning) but may have multiple Applications. There is a danger in preaching (and also in our private reading) of using the Bible as some sort of daily horoscope.

John Macarthur: 'Many well-meaning believers approach their Bibles with a high degree of subjectivity and mysticism. While they wouldn't admit to it, they read, study and apply Scripture as if any particular passage can almost any meaning at a particular time. For them, the Bible is a collection of sanctified fortune cookies. Break one open, read the verse, and figure out how it applies to what's happening in my life. The big question is, "What does this verse mean to me?" rather than the simpler, and much more important, "What does the verse mean?".

12 CONCLUSIONS
Finishing Well

The best messages build up to some fireworks at the finish. The conclusion must not be weak and wandering; it must force the issue, and 'clinch the sale'. Finish the message well, and end quickly. William Jennings Bryan's mother once told him, 'You missed several good opportunities to sit down'.

- Summarise the message; don't take too long doing this or it will not be a summary! Return to a question or issue raised earlier, repeating a striking phrase, or completing a story begun earlier.

- Move the listeners' will to act upon the message. The conclusion should include an exhortation, urging people to apply the message to their lives. However, do not leave all the application till the conclusion! Repeatedly point out the application of what you are talking about as you proceed through the sermon.

- Engage the heart in the conclusion. A conclusion should bring a message to its emotional climax; it should not end with an apologetic whimper. Maybe use some human interest story or testimony.

- 'Don't wind down as you are winding up your message' (Emily McLaren)

13 HELPFUL DELIVERY

A Speaker's Words and Actions Must Not Detract from the Message

Bryan Chappell: 'No set of delivery dos and don'ts supersedes the power of caring deeply about what you say. Let earnestness be your eloquence. Even if the words you say barely trip over the lip of the pulpit, if you speak with the sincerity of a burdened spirit, others will listen. Showing enthusiasm for what you deeply believe is the only unbreakable rule of delivery'.

- Be humble (Prov. 16:18, Luke 18:14), but not apologetic (1 Peter 4:11)
- Preach from the heart: 'The three essentials for great preaching are: truth, clarity and passion' (Campbell-Morgan)
- Gestures: use body language (Acts 21:40). 'God designed the human body to move. If your congregation wants to look at a statue, they can go to a museum' (Robinson).
- Avoid peculiar motions: the boxer (clenched fists, whirling arms), blacksmith (pounds the Bible), mannequin (no movement), thumb-twiddler (hands clasped, thumbs rotating), bird (flaps arms), heel-rocker, button-twirler.
- Eye-contact: 'the most effective means of non-verbal communication' (Robinson). Jesus 'lifted up his eyes toward his disciples' (as He delivered the Sermon on the Plain, Luke 6:20)
- Voice: speak up; 'then He opened His mouth and taught them' (Matt. 5:2). 'Open your mouth' is the first rule of public speaking.

How Long should I Preach?

Sermonettes make Christianettes. Do not give in to the demand for 15 minute messages. On the other hand, preaching time is shrinking. It used to be an hour. Now, you need to aim for 30-40 minutes max. If you preach too long, this is all people will remember. Try to cut down on any repetition, redundancy or irrelevant material.

One thing annoys people more than any other: going over time. Don't do it unless you are on fire! My grandfather used to say, 'the longer he spoke, the more they tyred'.

Section Three:

Studying the Bible in Preparation for Preaching

14 SPIRITUAL PRINCIPLES OF PREPARATION

THE BIG THREE ELEMENTS OF PREACHING

'Then Haggai the LORD's messenger spoke the LORD's message to the people' (Haggai 1:13). If Haggai's description is a good biblical definition of preaching, then the three most important elements of preaching are: (1) a message (i.e. one main idea), (2) from the Lord, which in our case means it is based on the Bible (i.e. biblical faithfulness), (3) delivered through the Lord's messenger (i.e. spiritual power).

HOW TO GET A MESSAGE FROM GOD

If preaching is a message from God, we preachers need to be busy doing three things:

1. We need to regularly read and obey the Bible ourselves. If we are not engaged in faithfully and regularly reading God's Word in private (not for preaching, but for fellowship with God), we are really going to struggle if we prepare a message for preaching. We need to develop a plan for regularly and systematically reading through the entire Bible. Only this way will we have the 'raw materials' for preaching. More than this, we need to be 'living' the Bible, so that we are filled with God's Spirit. We need to be applying it first to our own lives before preaching it to others.

2. We need to prayerfully meditate on the Bible, depending upon God's Spirit for help. The Holy Spirit is the Author of Scripture (2 Tim. 3:16), and the Interpreter of Christ (John 14:26, 16:13), the One who Reveals the truths of God (1 Cor. 2:9-16). Anything that grieves the Spirit (Eph. 4:30) will hinder us being taught by Him.

3. We need to hear God speaking to us from the Bible. R. T. Kendall wrote that, when he is studying the Bible for preaching, he is looking for 'insights'. Other people describe it as 'something that jumped off the page and hit them between the eyes'. Others will use less exciting spiritual language and instead say that 'this really spoke to me'. We need this conviction: God has spoken.

The long and the short of it is this: preaching is built upon certain spiritual disciplines. It is possible for some people to fake it, standing up in front of others and 'putting on a show', giving a motivational speech or a 'nice talk' or a dry biblical lecture, but there will be no spiritual power, nor truth brought out of the Word of God in a fresh and helpful way, nor any message from God that convicts and converts.

Some Suggestions:
- Clear away distractions in your life that 'choke the word' (Mark 4:19)
- The best way to spend quality personal time with God is early – before the mind becomes distracted
- Jot insights and ideas from God's Word down on paper – they can be developed later.
- Share the things that God shows you to encourage others – this aids memory (Mal. 3:16, Heb. 3:13)

CAUTIONS AND CAVEATS

1. Sometimes, you might only get the first glimpse of a truth in a passage, or the start of a message. Don't expect to always get a full three-point sermon dropped into your lap by God (although it sometimes happens!). Now you are on the scent of something good, but you are going to have to put in a lot more hard work, studying the passage, to flesh out the rest of your message.
2. It doesn't always have to be insights into God's Word that give you a foothold in a passage. Instead, it might sometimes be a problem or a question that you notice as you read God's Word. This problem is something that piques your interest, and provokes you to come back to the passage and study it more carefully. God sometimes leaves us clues like this to chase down.

GEORGE MULLER'S EXPERIENCE

'I fell into the snare into which so many young believers fall – the reading of religious books in preference to the Scriptures. I could no longer read French and German novels as I had formerly done to feed my carnal mind; but still I did not put in the place of those books the best of all books. I read tracts, missionary papers, sermons, and biographies of godly persons.

The last kind of books I found more profitable than the others, and had they been well selected, or had I not read too much of them, or had any of them served to endear the Scriptures to me, they might have done me much good. I had never been in the habit of reading the Holy Scriptures'.

'Now the scriptural way of reasoning would have been: God Himself has condescended to become an author, and I am ignorant about that precious Book, which His Holy Spirit has caused to be written through His servants, and it contains that which I ought to know to lead me to true happiness; therefore I ought to read this precious Book most earnestly, most prayerfully, and with much meditation; and in this I ought to continue all the days of my life . . .'

'But instead of acting thus, for the first four years of my divine life, I preferred the works of uninspired men to the oracles of the living God. In consequence I remained a baby, both in knowledge and in grace'. 'All true knowledge must be derived by the Spirit from the Word. And as I neglected the Word, I was for nearly four years so ignorant that I did not clearly know even the fundamental points of our holy faith. And this lack of knowledge most sadly kept me back from walking steadily in the ways of God. . .'

'When it pleased the Lord in August 1829 to bring me really to the Scriptures, my life and walk became very different. And though even since that I have very much fallen short of what I might and ought to be, I have been enabled to live much nearer to Him than before. . . If you understand very little of the Word of God, you ought to read it very much, for the Spirit explains the Word by the Word. And if you enjoy reading the Word little, that is just the reason why you should read it much, for the frequent reading of the Scripture creates a delight in them, so that the more we read them, the more we desire to do so...'

'When we read the Scriptures, it is of the greatest importance to meditate on what we read. . . . Learned commentaries I have found to store the head with many notions, and often also with the truth of God; but when the Spirit teaches, through the instrumentality of prayer and meditation, the heart is affected. The former kind of knowledge generally puffs up, and is often renounced when another commentary gives a different opinion, and often also is found to be good for nothing when it is put into practice. The latter kind of knowledge generally humbles, gives joy, leads us nearer to God, and thus having entered into the heart and become our own, is also generally carried out.'

'The Holy Spirit alone can teach us about our state by nature, show us the need of the Saviour, enable us to believe in Christ, explain to us the Scriptures, and help us in our preaching. It was my beginning to understand this latter point in particular, which had a great effect on me; for the Lord enabled me to put it to the test of experience, by laying aside commentaries, and almost every other book, and simply reading the Word of God and studying it.'

'The result of this was that the first evening I shut myself into my room to give myself to prayer and meditation over the Scriptures, I learned more in a few hours that I had done during a period of several months previously. But the particular difference was that I received real strength for my soul in doing so.'

15 MEDITATION

If the main ingredient of any sermon is a message from God (Haggai 1:13), what do you do if you don't have one? What if nothing is 'jumping out at you' from Scripture as you prepare to preach?

This is, in fact, usually the case. If you are teaching children the Scriptures, you need to prepare a new lesson every week from scratch, and you need a 'message'. If you lead a Bible study group, you need to have a message from the passage that you are helping your group to discover. If you are preaching regularly, particularly in a consecutive systematic context, you are often asked to preach on a passage that you aren't familiar with, or a passage that nothing seems to 'speak to you' from.

Some people today go and look on the internet for a sermon to use, or look for a sermon outline in books. This is shameful! A preacher should have a message that God has first taught him personally, before passing it on to others. This causes growth in dependance on God and fellowship with God.

So, how do you get 'the message', or (to use other language) determine the Big Idea of a passage or text? The answer involves a balance and tension between two concepts:

1. God's Holy Spirit illuminates Scripture – He shows you the 'message', but this happens as …
2. We Meditate on Scripture – we mull over the passage. (See Psalm 119:97-104)

How to Meditate on Scripture to Get a Message

We need to meditate on Scripture. It is very rarely the case that an entire 'message' will fall into our lap after we have casually read a passage once. So how do we meditate on Scripture for preaching? Matthew Henry said: 'Make the Bible your study. There is no knowledge, which I am more desirous to increase in, than that. Men get wisdom by books; but wisdom towards God is to be gotten out of God's book; and that by digging. Most men do but walk over the surface of it, and pick up here and there a flower.

Few dig into it. Read over other books to help you understand that book. Fetch your prayers and sermons from thence. The volume of inspiration is a full fountain, ever overflowing, and hath always something new' (quoted in Charles Bridges, *The Christian Ministry*, p51, fn. 1)

1. **Translate the Passage from the Original Language**. This is my preference for meditating on a passage for preaching, because it involves the most intense meditation, not only on the meaning of words and grammar, but also connections. <u>Advantages</u>: helps you to get behind familiar phraseology that dulls the senses, helps you meditate on every individual word, helps you to notice connections between words in the original language repeated elsewhere in the passage but obscured by English synonyms. <u>Disadvantages</u>: This method takes more time than some other methods of meditating. This method also only works if you are familiar with the original language, although it might be possible to do something similar by using an interlinear and a Hebrew/Greek lexicon, but you need to know the alphabet and a basic understanding of grammar to find the words in these lexicons.
2. **Read the Passage through in a Number of Different English translations**: This is essential if you have no way of studying the passage in the original language. By reading different translations (use more literal ones), you will get behind familiar phraseology, and you might also pick up some verbal connections obscured in one translation. You will need to note down differences between translations that can be later investigated more thoroughly in your Word Study preparation.
3. **Paraphrase the Passage**: Go down through the passage, and write out each verse in your own words. This causes you to think carefully about the passage. This is a good method for teaching Religious Instruction in schools or Sunday School.
4. **Question the Passage**: Write out a question (or two) about every verse in the passage. This again causes you to think about every verse. This also helps you to think about practical application.
5. **Brainstorm the Passage**: as you read down through the passage, note

down anything that comes to mind – a question about some verse, a key word that crops up, an application that might suggest itself. This is the least valuable way of meditating, because it can be quite shallow and quick.

As we continue to turn over the passage in our minds, the message, a.k.a. the Big Idea, will become clearer. Only by doing some sort of meditation like this will we have the 'raw materials' for preaching. But there remains much preparation work still to be done. This is only stage one of study preparation.

16 THE BIG IDEA AND STRUCTURE

So far, in Studying the Bible for Preaching, we have argued that we need two things:

1. A message from the Lord – our task is spiritual, and we must wait upon God
2. To meditate deeply upon God's Word – this is our responsibility for the task

We listed five possible ways of meditation: translating, reading multiple translations, paraphrasing, questioning and brainstorming. Assuming that we use a combination of these methods, and we now have a page of densely scribbled notes going down through the passage, what do we do next?

THE NEXT STEP: SUMMARY AND DIVISION

Firstly, we try to synthesize all of these notes and thoughts together into a simple summary, distilling all of the information before us into one central theme: the Big Idea. Another way of trying to work out the Big Idea is to ask ourselves this question: What precisely is the biblical author talking about? The Big Idea can be either a statement or question, e.g. Reasons to praise the Lord vs Why praise the Lord?

Secondly, we try to divide the passage up according to the main sub-divisions that occur in it. These will usually be paragraph divisions in epistles or narratives. Alternatively, we might occasionally notice a number of themes that occur through the passage and look upon these as the main thoughts, even if they do not correspond precisely with the paragraph divisions of the passage. Within these sub-divisions, again, we try to summarize these paragraphs or ideas, so that now we have one Big Idea and several sub-ideas. Together, these make up the skeleton of our message.

There are two ways to work out the Big Idea and Structure: Big Idea first or structure first. Sometimes it will not be easy to boil everything down into one Big Idea straight away, and instead we work from the ground up, looking for natural divisions and summarising these paragraphs, before trying to see what is the central theme that these separate sub-headings all connect to, like spokes to a hub on a wheel.

To work out the Big Idea, we look for connections – words or ideas that are repeated (a method of emphasising these ideas) or related. Different methods for marking up these connections include:
- on our page of notes, circle or underline these words and then connect them with lines.
- photocopy the page of the Bible and mark up our connections using coloured highlighters.
- another alternative is to make a separate list of key words for the passage, noting where they occur.

The same applies to the individual paragraphs – we look for and mark up connections. On the other hand, for divisions, we look for contrasts in theme – we notice where groups of words/themes change.

17 SERMON SUMMARY STATEMENT

A Sermon Summary Statement (SSS) is a good way to see (1) if you have really understood the passage you are preaching on and (2) that you have got a clear idea of how to preach it. A SSS contains two parts. Just as all sentences have a subject and a predicate, so too an SSS has a Subject and Complement:

Subject	Predicate
I	went to the shops
The Gospel	is the power of God to salvation

We can see from these examples that the subject is the main person, thing, or idea in a sentence, while the predicate is whatever completes the sentence, which is usually everything from the verb onwards in the sentence. The predicate tells us something about the subject.

THE SUBJECT: THE BIG IDEA OF THE PASSAGE

Firstly, the SSS has a subject. The subject in an SSS is our **Big Idea**. For example, we might preach from Ephesians 2:1-10 and say that the subject (or Big Idea) is How we are Saved. The Subject (or Big Idea) doesn't have to be one word. For example, in John 1:1-18, the Big Idea is Jesus is the Word of God.

Sometimes our Big Idea might be too broad and vague. For example, we might think that the Big Idea of James 1:5-8 ('if any of you lacks wisdom, let him ask God', etc.) is 'wisdom'. However, a better answer is that James is not talking about wisdom generally. Instead, as we see from the context in verses 2-4 (which are about trials) we could say that the Big idea is: How we obtain wisdom in the midst of trials.

THE PREDICATE: WHAT THE PASSAGE TEACHES US ABOUT THE BIG IDEA

In the case of James 1:5-8, the predicate is: 'ask for it in faith'. The entire SSS is therefore: We obtain wisdom in the midst of trials by asking for it in faith'. In the case of Ephesians 2, the complement is (a) as sinners (vs1-

3), (b) by God grace (vs4-7), (c) by faith not works (vs8-10). The complete SSS is: We are saved as sinners by God's grace through faith. In John 1:1-18 the complement is: (a) Jesus is truly God (vs1-5), (b) Jesus is far greater than any man, like John the Baptist (vs6-8), (c) Jesus came into the world as a man (vs10-18). From these last two examples, we see the value of the predicate/complement: they often correspond to a 'clear structure'.

The SSS for John 1:1-18 is 'Jesus, the Word of God, is truly God, far greater than any man, yet become truly human'. Putting everything into a SSS helps you to clarify if your Big Idea really relates to your main points, and whether you have correctly identified the Big Idea. Having a SSS forces you to think more carefully about how your Big Idea relates to the complement - i.e. your Clear Structure.

Let us take another example, from 1 Corinthians 13. We might initially think that, for 1 Corinthians 13, the subject is love. However, perhaps a better Big Idea (i.e. a more *exact* subject) here is this: Love is Superior to Spiritual Gifts. But the predicate fleshes this out for you in the sort of detail that is required for preaching.

Subject   Predicate
Love is more (a) profitable, (b) practical (c) and permanent than spiritual gifts

You need not use the a, b, c notation in your sermon statement – these are included here to help you notice that the sub-divisions vs 1-3, 4-7, 8-13 come from, and correspond to, the chapter itself. Forming a sermon statement (a) helps us to get our message clear, and (b) gives us a target for our study.

18 FILLING OUT THE SERMON

Once you have a Big Idea and a Clear Structure, how do you fill out your sermon?

Having a clear structure is not enough. You will have to do more than simply announce it and proceed to your conclusion. Often your audience won't accept what you are preaching without further help. There are seven things that you will often have to do when you preach.

1. You will have to **state** your (new) point,

2. You need to **ground** (or reference) your point from the text by reading out the words in the passage that back our point up.

3. You might have to **explain** a truth (e.g., in 1 Corinthians 8, we might ask, What does it mean when it talks about the weaker brother?), or,

4. You might need to **prove** something is true (e.g. non-Christians might not accept that sin is serious and dangerous).

5. We might have to **illustrate** the truth (for a variety of reasons).

6. We should **apply** the truth, by showing what difference it makes to our lives.

Which one of these approaches we use will depend on the passage and the needs of the audience. After we explain and/or prove, illustrate and/or apply the truth,

7. We can use a **transition** to move to our next point.

19 EMPHASIS, ORDER AND CONTEXT

As we have seen a number of times, the most important thing to have in a sermon is a message, or (as we call it) a Big Idea. We must wait upon God for it, but also meditate. In a previous chapter we looked at one way to try and find the big idea – by looking for connections – repeated ideas in a passage that collectively spell out the main theme. But sometimes the key idea is not repeatedly mentioned in a passage, nor is it even always spelled out explicitly in words. What other ways are there to try to identify the Big Idea?

EMPHASIS

Bible writers did not use a different font style to emphasise key ideas – like boldface or italic. So if there is a key idea that they wish to emphasise, how do they do it?

One way that biblical writers emphasise their main point is just to tell you their main purpose. For example, 1 John 5:13 says, 'These things I have written to you who believe in the name of the Son of God, that you may know that you have eternal life'. John 20:31 says, 'these [things] are written that you may believe that Jesus is the Christ, the Son of God, and that believing you may have life in His name'. Hebrews 8:1 says, 'Now this is the main point of the things we are saying: We have such a High Priest, who is seated at the right hand of the throne of the Majesty in the heavens'. The book of Proverbs starts with a purpose statement in Proverbs 1:2-7, 'To know wisdom and instruction, To perceive the words of understanding, To receive the instruction of wisdom, Justice, judgment, and equity, etc.'.

Another way that the NT emphasises something is to either drag a word to the front of a sentence or leave it till last (Greek word order is very free and fluid). This might not always show up in English translations. For example, (lit.) '**God's** fellow workers we are; **God's** field you are, **God's** building' (1 Cor. 3:9). The Corinthians were squabbling and divided, but needed to be reminded Who owned the church. Paul's point is that the church not only belongs to God, but He is the One who gives the growth.

Use an interlinear to check out the Greek word order.

Another way that emphasis is conveyed in the Bible is by the order of events. Matthew and Luke have a different order of events in Christ's temptation. In fact, both start with the temptation to turn bread into stone, which only happened at the end of the 40 days when Christ was hungry. But they swap the order of the other two temptations. Matthew's Gospel culminates in the offer of all the kingdoms of the world – a messianic temptation, where Luke's gospel climaxes with the 'throw yourself down' temptation – in keeping with Luke's moral focus on Christ as the Perfect Man.

CONTEXT

Often it helps to look at the surrounding context to determine the main point. Stories before or after our passage provide connections and contrasts that help us to see what is being taught. Examples:

1. The four miracles that Mark and Luke give one after the other – stilling the storm, Legion's demons cast out, the woman with the haemorrhage and Jairus' daughter. The placement of these stories emphasises certain things by repetition: Christ's power, people's faith and salvation.
2. The story of Zaccheus (Luke 19) is preceded by other stories that are connected by the idea of people being saved (parable of Pharisee and Tax-collector, rich young ruler, Bartimaeus). But another connection is that a lot of these stories have to do with money, while Zaccheus provides a contrast in that while Christ said that rich people will find it hard to be saved (Luk 18:24), Zaccheus is saved even though he is rich.
3. What is the point of the story of Judah's terrible sins of immorality in Genesis 38? Some argue that this tells us about salvation-history and Christ's line of descent. But the contrast between Judah's sexual sins and Joseph's refusal to be tempted by Potiphar's wife in Gen. 39 is more likely the contextual reason (notice the way coats are important 'props' in both stories).

20 ASKING THE RIGHT QUESTIONS

One of the ways it is possible to meditate on Scripture in preparation for preaching is to ask questions of the text. This helps us to think about the passage in a number of different ways.

QUESTIONS WE CAN ASK

Rudyard Kipling famously said: 'I have six honest serving men, they taught me all I knew, their names are What and Where and When, and Why and How and Who'. Here are some of the different questions we can ask as we meditate on the Bible:

Background Questions

- Who was writing this? To whom was it originally written?
- When was it written? Where was it written?

To answer these background questions, we need to read the entire book we are studying, and sometimes other books in the Bible that provide more background information.

Content Questions

- What is happening in this verse? What is being stated in this verse?
- What are the key words or phrases used in this passage? What is the meaning of this word?
- What type of literature is this (Poetry, narrative, parable, letter)? What difference does this make?
- What is the main point of this passage?

Interpretation Questions

- What does this mean? How can we reconcile this verse with other verses in the Bible?

Three Important Preaching Questions

Haddon Robinson in his book *Biblical Preaching* argues that it is important that, as we preach, that we answer three important questions:

1. What does this mean? Our job as preachers is to explain the text. We need to put ourselves in our listeners' shoes, anticipate what they do not know, and try to help them to understand the passage.
2. Is it true? We must prove that God's Word is true and can be believed. Even Bible writers prove their points by using arguments, evidence, illustrations, experience and examples.
3. What difference does it make? Our job is also to apply Scripture to people's lives today.

THE MOST IMPORTANT QUESTION: WHY?

One of the most important questions we can ask is, What is the Main Point of this passage. This helps us to understand the Big Idea, or Main Message that we will preach on. However, perhaps even more important than this is the question, **Why was this written?** What was the **Author's Original Intention?** This question brings together many of the other background and contextual questions (raised earlier), shows us the Main Message, and helps us see how to apply the Bible to our lives today.

Examples: Why was **1 Cor. 13** written? Context (chapters 12 and 14) shows us that Paul is not composing a love-poem for Christian weddings, but showing that spiritual gifts (e.g. tongues) need to be used in ways which build up others. Why was **1 Thess. 1** written? Paul rehearses the Thessalonians' conversion in Ch. 1 because (as Ch. 3 shows), they were persecuted. Paul wants to assure them of the genuineness of their conversion so they will continue to grow in their faith and not be discouraged. From these examples, we see it helps to look at the context. Passages before or after our text provide connections and contrasts that help us to see what, and more imporantly, **why** it is being taught.

21 WORD STUDIES

One of the most important tasks in Bible study is looking carefully at the meaning of words.

STEP ONE: WHAT WORDS TO STUDY

We should study any words: 1. That we do not understand, or are ambiguous 2. Where translations diverge, 3. That are rare and unusual, 4. That appear to be pivotal for the understanding of the text.

STEP TWO: LOOK UP AN ENGLISH DICTIONARY

If we do not understand an English word, we can look up an English dictionary. We can also look up an expository dictionary, in which we look up our English words to trace the meaning of the underlying Greek or Hebrew words. Two examples are *Vine's Expository Dictionary of NT Words* and Spiros Zodhiates *The Complete Word Study Dictionary*. These can give a helpful start to word studies.

STEP THREE: LOOK UP A GREEK OR HEBREW LEXICON

For proper word studies, we need to get beyond English translations and dictionaries. We can track down the original (e.g. Greek) word by using a Greek NT, or an interlinear (the best is Newberry's – in U.S, it is called George Ricker Berry's). One benefit of looking here is that we can see where the same Greek word is used throughout a passage, because often English Bibles hide this repetition and connection by using synonyms. E.g. in John 5, the KJV uses 'judgment', 'condemnation' and 'damnation', but the same Greek word underlies each. Also, we can look up the English word in a concordance, and use the Strong's numbers to look up the Greek dictionary section at the back. Once we have found the correct Greek or Hebrew word, we need to look up a lexicon. To do this, we will need to know the Greek or Hebrew alphabet to track down a word. A lexicon shows the **range of meanings** a Greek or Hebrew word takes. The best Greek lexicon is BDAG (Bauer Danker Arndt Gingrich), although Abbott-Smith is good too. Liddell-Scott is the standard Classical Greek lexicon – it shows how a word was used in the period before the NT, giving some historical background.

STEP FOUR: LOOK AT ALL THE REFERENCES

Once we have noted the range of meanings a word takes, we need to look at every occurrence of a word. My preferred NT Greek lexicon is Abbott-Smith, primarily because it does not try to do what BDAG does – list all the various (sometimes artificial) subdivisions of meaning. i.e. Abbott-Smith forces you to work through all the occurrences of a word in the NT and think about what it means in context. Again, looking at all the occurrences helps us to see what different meanings a word takes in different settings.

STEP FIVE: LOOK AT THE IMMEDIATE CONTEXT

Lastly, we need to look at the context of the word, and see which of the possible meanings fits the context best. This is the exact opposite of just picking the meaning that suits our theology or purpose.

Examples: The word 'world' is a translation of different Greek words: *kosmos* (John 3:16), *aion* (= 'age', Rom. 12:2) and *oikoumene* (= 'inhabited (area)', i.e. the 'Roman world', Luke 2:1). Eph. 4:19 says unbelievers give themselves to 'lasciviousness' (KJV), 'lewdness' (NKJV), 'sensuality' (NIV, ESV, NAS), 'licentiousness' (NRSV). The Greek word *aselgeia* is defined by BDAG as 'licentiousness, debauchery, sensuality', but by Liddell-Scott just as 'licentiousness'. Does the word carry a sexual connotation in Eph. 4:19? Abbott-Smith lists 10 references in the NT, and only in some is there a sexual association (Rom. 13:13, 2 Cor. 12:21, Gal. 5:19); others do not (e.g. Mark 7:22, Jude 4). It seems best to treat it as a more general issue – 'licentiousness, no restraint' – that is not confined to sexual sins. Or consider *hairesis*, translated 'heresies' in 2 Pet. 2:1, but 'sect' in Acts 24:5, 14, etc. The word can either refer to a false opinion, or the party that unites around that belief. In Titus 3:10, is a 'heretic' (KJV) or a 'divisive man' (NKJV) to be rejected? Probably, from context (v9), a divisive person who persists in quarrelling.

22 STRUCTURE

God has given us His Word in whole books, not in encyclopedia or dictionary form (with alphabetical entries), nor in systematic theology form (with major topics in systematic order), nor in chapters and verses (these divisions are not inspired). Therefore, we must seek to understand how these 66 inspired books – many of which are too long to read in one sitting – are arranged.

In the last chapter we saw the importance of word studies. Each word is inspired and important. But we also need to zoom out and try to understand where a passage fits into the structure of its book. This can often be helpful in understanding the point of the passage, and its purpose in the book we are studying.

EXAMPLES OF STRUCTURE IN BIBLE BOOKS

Genesis is clearly structured – it has narratives interspersed with genealogies. Genesis also uses the word 'generations, histories' (Heb. *toledoth*) to highlight these divisions. The first six sections show God's judgment, while the last six sections relate God's blessing through Abraham's family. The narratives are (mostly) centred on individuals: Adam, Noah, Abraham, Joseph, etc., and the plot-line of the book reaches its conclusion in the salvation that Joseph brings to the world, a little picture of Christ. In the NT, **John's Gospel** has two main sections (and other 'sub-sections' too). Chapters 1-12 show us Christ coming to 'His own' (1:11), the Jewish people. Despite the signs, Israel do not believe. Chapters 13-21 show us Christ's love for 'His own' (13:1) – the disciples, and the way we are to live as His people.

STRUCTURAL ELEMENTS AND INDICATORS

- <u>Summary statements</u>: in the book of Acts, different sections conclude with similar statements about the growth and spread of the gospel: Acts 6:7, 12:24-5, 19:20, etc. In the books of Samuel and Kings we see the same, e.g. 1 Sam. 7:15-17 (Samuel), 2 Sam. 8:15-18 (David's officials), 1 Kings 4 (Solomon's reign).

- <u>Marker elements</u>: in Luke's Gospel, different sections in the second half of the book have 'journey markers' noted as Jesus moves towards Jerusalem: Luke 10:38, 13:22, 17:11, etc.
- <u>Different Blocks</u>: often, different sections have distinct content or even different types of content, e.g. blocks of narratives interspersed with sermons in Matthew's gospel.

HELPFULNESS OF STRUCTURE

Structure shows that God's word is wisely put together. More specifically, structure can show us the purpose of a book. For example, **Leviticus** has sections dealing with sacrifices and priests (Chs 1-10), cleanliness (Chs 11-15) and holiness (Chs 16-27). These sections follow the way into the presence of God as symbolised in the Tabernacle, with its altar, laver and 'holy places' (Exodus Chs 25-40). We therefore need to learn to read Scritpure macroscopically – looking at the 'big picture' of books.

DANGERS OF STRUCTURE

While structure can be very helpful in helping us to see the purpose of a book, it also presents dangers. Sometimes, our 'structures' are our own invented and imaginary structures rather than the design of the inspired author. Our 'structures' are no more inspired than our chapter divisions. To base weighty arguments upon them is therefore precarious. For example, some argue that **Luke-Acts** presents a chiastic (X-shaped) structure: Luke starts with Jesus' birth set in the context of the Roman world, and proceeds with Jesus' ministry in Galilee, Samaria, Judea and Jerusalem, while Acts moves in the opposite direction: Jerusalem, Judea, Samaria, Roman world. At the centre of the chiastic structure is Jesus' death and resurrection. All very good, but one problem is that Luke's Gospel does not start with Caesar in Rome, but with Zechariah the priest in the temple in Jerusalem. Finding faults with such structures shows they are maybe more 'imposed' than inspired.

23 HELPS AND BOOKS

Here is some advice regarding books and helps in preparation and study for preaching.

God's Word and God's Spirit

It is possible to prepare for preaching just using our Bible, depending prayerfully on the Holy Spirit. God's Word and Spirit are the essential ingredients for a message from God, and substituting any human books for them is a recipe for failure. However, the Bible was not originally written in English, so if we can read the Bible in Hebrew and Greek, we are less likely to mistake the meaning of the words God uses. Moreover, it is important to read all of God's Word, not only our favourite books or verses.

It is important to do our own study, depending on God for the message, before we look at other books and helps. The exception to this is looking for help to understand word meanings.

Word Helps

As mentioned in the previous lesson, it is important to get a Concordance (Young's, Strong's, Cruden's) to find where words are used in the Bible. Topical conconcordances like *Nave's* trace topics throughout the Bible. Bible dictionaries are like encyclopedias listing topics. For information about words, consult *Vine's Expository Dictionary of NT Words* or Spiros Zodhiates *The Complete Word Study Dictionary*. Use an interlinear like *The Englishman's Greek New Testament* (George Ricker Berry in the USA) to track down Greek words. The best Greek lexicon is BDAG (Bauer Danker Arndt Gingrich), although Abbott-Smith is good too, and Thayer's is helpful. For Hebrew, use Holladay, Gesenius, or Brown, Driver and Briggs.

Grammar

Of almost equal importance to word studies are grammar studies, looking at the way words are used in sentences. For example, does Rom. 3:22 speak of the 'righteousness of God' (NKJV) or the 'righteousness from God' (NIV)? Is it talking about a characteristic of God, or something God gives to us? Commentaries will help with grammar, learning the language is even better, but ultimately, you need to look to God to help you understand the author's original intention, by considering the context.

COMMMENTARIES

After we have done our own study and got our message, it is useful to look at commentaries to check our understanding of the passage we are studying. There are different levels of commentaries:

- **One volume commentaries**: William MacDonald's *Believers' Bible Commentary*, John *MacArthur's Bible Commentary*, Zondervan Bible Commentary (mostly Brethren writers), the New Bible Commentary (IVP), Matthew Henry (devotional and practical)
- **Expository commentaries** (good for preaching, more detailed than above): The *Tyndale* OT & NT Commentaries, the *Bible Speaks Today* commentaries, *Focus on the Bible* commentaries
- **Technical commentaries** (dealing with the Greek and Hebrew text, expensive): NIGTC (New international Greek Testament Commentary), NICNT/OT (New International Commentary on the NT/OT, Baker Exegetical Commentary, *Pillar* (less technical, no knowledge of Greek required)

COMPUTER AND ONLINE RESOURCES

Nowadays we have many computer Bibles. You can also read many commentaries online (e.g 110 on Studylight). The best free computer Bible is probably *E-sword*, or *The Word*. These have lots of free Bible versions, commentaries, dictionaries, etc. There are many computer Bibles you can buy, but for serious word studies, use Bibleworks or Accordance. For building up a library of commentaries, use Logos (very expensive). Beware of investing too heavily in computer Bible resources – companies go out of business(e.g. Bibleworks) and technologies get superseded. Lastly, do not become part of a Youtube cult!

24 SERMON PREPARATION TIMETABLE

Here is a suggested outline including a rough timetable for preparing your sermon. Allow a good 10 hours. (Some famous preachers put twice as much time as this into their sermon preparation). Remember: Preaching requires more than a few thoughts that come to a man while waiting in a bus queue.

MEDITATION AND PRAYER (2 HOURS)

- Pray
- Read the passage itself repeatedly. Use different Bible translations, noting differences
    - ALTERNATIVELY: Translate the passage from the original language if you are able.
- Study the passage line by line, meditating (i.e. reading carefully and prayerfully) upon its words and what they are meant to teach. Keep a notepad handy, and jot down any things that come to mind during this process: any insights, questions, apparent problems, practical applications, suggestions for main ideas.

ANALYSIS OF PASSAGE (3 HOURS)

- <u>Analyze the Passage</u>: look for <u>connections</u> in the passage (i.e. words or ideas that link up throughout), and look at the <u>Structure</u> of the passage: where the paragraph (or other) divisions are. Try and map out an idea of the <u>Flow of the argument</u> and thought.
- <u>Analyze the Context</u>: Read the larger context, including the passage (e.g. epistle or section of epistle, surrounding chapters of gospel, OT book, etc). Look for any connections and contrasts in text and context.
- <u>Do Word Studies</u>. Notice any verses where there are different words in more literal translations (e.g. NKJV, ESV, NASB). Use dictionaries or concordances, or computer Bibles to look at the Greek/Hebrew words, and check the Greek or Hebrew definitions to get a good idea of their meaning.

- Make a list of Key Words or themes. Look out for commonly repeated words in the passage, noting where they are found. These may help identify the big idea of main themes.
- Investigate Cross-references to other verses that may help you understand (use Bible marginal references)
- Ask the WHY question: what is the Point of the Passage? Look at the 'backstory' (reasons that might have prompted an epistle, or the historical situation), to try to work out the relevance for the original readers.
- Identify any Doctrinal issues: does this passage confirm (or clarify or appear to clash with) any truths (about God, Christ, the Holy Spirit, sin, salvation, etc.), found elsewhere in the Bible?
- Application: What possible lessons for our life today might arise from the text?
- Reference Books: Investigate any historical or cultural issues, using a Bible encyclopedia or dictionary, and check some commentaries for what the passage means.

SERMON PREPARATION (2 HOURS)

- Identify the Big Idea, or Main Message of your passage.
- Try to put together a Clear Structure. This is the main outline of your message (i.e. your sermon 'points'), and will be based either on the main sub-divisions of a passage, or its main thoughts that tell us what the passage is saying about the Big Idea. This may take a lot of time, struggling to get this right.
- Check your Big Idea and Structure using a Sermon Summary Sentence to check if they both go together naturally: The SSS is a grammatical sentence with a Subject (the Big Idea) and Complement (i.e. the Clear Structure: what the passage says about the Big idea – your sermon 'points').
- Think of some possible Applications
- Find some good Illustrations. If none come easily pray for the Lord to help you find them as you prepare.
- Consider the Introduction and Conclusion.

WRITE OUR YOUR MESSAGE (3 HOURS)

- <u>Write out your Sermon</u> in full.
- Either write out a <u>Sermon Outline in note form</u>, or <u>Mark up your written Sermon</u> manuscript with highlighter pen and marginal notes. Rehearse the preaching of it, correcting the manuscript and improving the sermon as a result of sentences that flow better as you practice preaching.

25 PREPARING FOR DELIVERING SERMONS

There are different opinions among preachers about the best way to deliver the sermon. Some write it out in full, some just use outline notes, and some even memorise the entire sermon.

Advantages and Disadvantages of Writing out your message in full:

- The advantages of writing out your sermon in full are (1) you can know roughly how long your sermon will be by this measure, so you can cut things out (or put them in), (2) you will be able to make sure you do not wander far from the topic, but stick to the script, (3) on sensitive topics you can get your wording just right, so you don't offend people or say things in a way that is not clear, (4) you have a written record of your sermon so you can use the notes to help you study the Bible in the future (DANGER: never simply repeat a sermon!).
- However, it is most important to remember that the power of a sermon does not consist in nicely-turned phrases, or splendid vocabulary. The power comes from a Spirit-filled speaker fit to teach God's Word.
- Another disadvantage of writing out a sermon is that you might be tempted to read it out. Do NOT do this! If you read out your sermon, you do not have as much eye-contact. Look people in the eye. 'Eye contact probably ranks as the single most effective means of non-verbal communication at your disposal' (H. Robinson). Further, if you read out your sermon, your tone of voice will also be very monotonous. This is very bad. 'It is to commit ministerial suicide by harping on one string' (Spurgeon). You need to use emotion in your message. You need to let people feel that you are talking to them, not just reading an academic lecture.
- Preaching is 'truth poured through personality' (P. Brooks), 'logic on fire (M. Lloyd-Jones). You have to let your personality shine through. Reading the sermon means you do not use body-language and gestures in your preaching. 'God designed the body to move. If your congregation wants to look at a statue, they can go to a museum' (H. Robinson). There was a man who went through Bible college with a

quiet student and some years later went to a big conference where, to his surprise, this quiet student was the dynamic speaker up the front. He went and spoke to him and found out his fellow-student realised that he needed to come out of himself to be a good preacher. Do not hide behind a pulpit – many modern preachers use a glass lectern, and move all over the stage. The best preachers have got a big personality. 'Be yourself, but bigger' (M. Raiter). Be natural, spontaneous and instinctive in your movements and gestures, not repetitive or robotic.
- There is an old saying: 'Study yourself full, write yourself clear, pray yourself hot, and preach yourself empty'.

Advantages and Disadvantages of Preaching from Notes:
- Notes take less time to prepare and mean you preach with more freedom and personality.
- But they also mean that you have not put as much time into the actual words of your sermon. Sometimes, the result is that unless the sermon has got lots of points (in note form), you might not have much to say (because you have not fleshed out your points). Your language might also be stale and tired, with lots of clichés, umms and ahhs.
- One of the big problems with preaching from notes is that a preacher will repeat his sentences two or three different ways to try and get the right words or to emphasise the importance of his point. This is very tiresome for listeners! It could have been avoided if he had put in the effort and written out his message in full so that he used just the right words to make and emphasize his points.

Memorise it?
- Some preachers write out their sermon in full, then memorise it, so that they are not tied to reading a manuscript. However, memorising takes a lot more time in preparation. Preaching is not a performance.
- Rehearsing you sermon beforehand? 'The music team rehearses, so should you' (M. Raiter).

The Best Solution
I suggest the best solution is to write out your sermon in full, and then either (1) make a separate set of notes from it, rehearse it and preach from

the notes, or else (2 – my preference) mark up your manuscript (with pen or highlighter) so that its main points stand out (as if it were notes), then rehearse it, and take it with you to preach inside the page of your Bible, but just glance at it as you proceed (Do NOT read it!).

If you read a passage of Scripture, and get a whole message jump right off the page at you, you can write it out in note form and preach it while it is still fresh in your mind. These are the best sermons – piping hot.

SECTION FOUR:

Preaching Different Types of Sermons

26 TOPICAL PREACHING

Topical preaching is preaching on a topic or subject, as opposed to preaching on a passage of Scripture.

BENEFITS AND DANGERS OF TOPICAL PREACHING

Some Christians are very keen on topical preaching. They think that if a topic or subject is announced, it will be more popular or more interesting than just preaching on a passage of Scripture. Some other Christians reject topical preaching and insist that all preaching should be expository preaching on passages. The truth is this: we need both expository preaching on passages and topical preaching. We need preaching that scrutinises Bible books passage by passage (microscopically), and topical preaching that synthesises what the whole Bible says on various topics (macroscopically).

The benefits of topical preaching are that we can address doctrinal (e.g. the Holy Spirit) or practical subjects (e.g. prayer) that are found scattered throughout the Bible rather than in just one location. We can 'connect the dots' and build up a systematic understanding on these subjects. Sometimes these topics might have immediate relevance, or might even be a 'word from God that meets the need of the moment', while it is true that some consecutive preaching can become dry, academic and irrelevant.

One danger of too frequent topical preaching on 'popular' or 'relevant' topics is that it can result in Christians without a broad knowledge of Scripture. Without the foundation of expository treatments of Bible books, preaching may lack the quarry of material that can be brought together in a topical message, resulting in constant preaching on the same theme, or (worse) on hobby-horses or eccentric ideas or teaching truths in a biblically unbalanced way. The desire for 'practical' preaching is good, but unless it is based upon, and balanced by, doctrinal truths (as in NT letters), it will produce lop-sided Christians. If there is a lack of expository preaching, carefully dealing with the text in context, Christians may also be less aware when Scripture is being distorted (or unbalanced) in topical preaching that pushes a particular agenda. Another danger of topical preaching is that it can become sensationalist, trying too hard to attract interest with racy subjects, instead of patiently trusting in the Word of God to work in peoples' lives. Another problem with topical preaching is that there are only so many subjects or topics to preach on, whereas expository preaching affords almost endless opportunities for a lifetime of preaching.

HOW TO PREACH ON TOPICS

1. It is obviously necessary to look at all that the Bible says on the subject. We need to trace the topic throughout the whole Bible. Sometimes, what the Bible teaches on a subject may be found in one main passage (e.g. new birth in John 3), and this helps to simplify matters. It is also important to have a clear structure for topical preaching to help listeners follow the message.
2. One good way to preach on topics is to ask questions about the subject. For example, on the subject of the New Birth, we can ask What (is it), Who needs it, Why, and How are we born again, etc.
3. Another way to preach on some topics is to look at the topic logically. For example, How do we know that God exists? Put the reasons in logical order: because of Creation, Conscience, Christ, etc.
4. Another approach is to preach controversial topics inductively. This is the opposite of deductive preaching where we state our position at the outset and fill out our reasons. Inductive preaching asks e.g. what is the mode of baptism and (rather than put off people) comes to an answer at the end.
5. Some other subjects may be traced throughout Scripture. For example, we can look at the person and work of the Holy Spirit in the OT, Life of Christ, book of Acts, and in the Letters.
6. Topical preaching needs introductions, applications and illustrations. Doctrines can be applied, and practical preaching should touch on doctrinal reasons (e.g. prayer: the nature of God).

27 TEXTUAL PREACHING

Textual preaching is preaching on just one verse of Scripture.

BENEFITS AND DANGERS OF TEXTUAL PREACHING

Textual preaching has been one of the most common and powerful types of preaching in Christian history, particularly in times when people didn't carry their Bibles to church. It can be argued that Paul's letter to the Romans is an exposition of one text: 'the just by faith shall live' (Hab. 2:4, cf. Rom. 1:17). One of the disadvantages of this sort of sermon, however, is this: it does not encourage Christians to gain a broad understanding of Scripture beside isolated texts. The surrounding contexts of favourite verses are left unexplored, and the contents of whole books of the Bible are left unexplained. Too much of this sort of preaching therefore has led to Christians being ignorant of their Bibles. On the other hand, one of the main ways that textual preaching has been usefully employed has been in evangelistic preaching, where non-Christians are not expected to have any prior knowledge of Bible books, or much interest in the background or context of gospel verses. Trying to help non-Christians gain a greater understanding of Bible books is not what the gospel preacher is aiming to do. Such information is beside the point of gospel preaching. The listener's atttention must be grabbed and the point directly made: the need and the way of salvation. Textual preaching thus cuts straight to the chase. Textual preaching also has this advantage: it is simple, and there is the possibility to repeatedly press home the application. One other advantage is that it helps listeners to easily remember the Bible's words that are preached upon. A type of textual sermon is to deal with a number of related texts that handle the same word of subject. This approach is good for beginning preachers who may not feel able to preach at length or in depth upon just one verse, but may helpfully speak briefly upon a number of related verses, and still bring across the gospel or the truths that the Word of God is presenting. One danger of this, however, is that it encourages a shallow approach to expounding the words of Scripture. It is good to move on from this.

HOW TO PREACH ON TEXTS AND EXAMPLES OF THIS

The normal features of preaching apply. There must be a Main Theme or

Big Idea of the sermon. If we are preaching the gospel, the main theme is obviously going to be something related to salvation. There must also be divisions or structure to our message. There are, as usual, a variety of types of divisions:

1. Sometimes it may be possible to take the individual words of the text as our divisions, and to emphasise these, maybe with titles. C. I. Scofield's message on John 10:9 was titled 'Seven facts regarding Salvation', divided as follows: (1) the Illustration of Salvation (I am the door), (2) the Personification of S. (by me), (3) the Invitation of S. (if any man), (4) the Qualification of S. (enter in), (5) the Possession of S. (he shall be saved), (6) the Emancipation of S. (and shall go in and out), (7) the Satisfaction of S. (and find pasture). Scofield used other NT verses to prove his points.
2. Another option is to use a logical progression. For example, 1 Tim. 1:15 teaches (1) We are sinners (Christ Jesus came into the world to save *sinners*), (2) we need to be saved (Christ Jesus came into the world to *save* sinners), (3) Christ is the Saviour (*Christ Jesus* came into the world to save sinners), (4) we must believe this and accept Him to be saved (this is a *faithful* saying and worthy of all *acceptance*). The context in 1 Tim. 1 helps to fill out the sermon: Paul's use of the Law convinces us of our guilt.
3. Spurgeon's 'greatest sermon' (aged 24) was on 'Compel them to come in' (Luke 14:23). His main divisions were (1) I must find you out (the poor, maimed, halt, blind, in highways and hedges) and (2) I must compel you to come in (I must tell, command, exhort, entreat, threaten, weep, appeal to the Spirit). Read at www.spurgeon.org/resource-library/sermons/compel-them-to-come-in/

28 CHARACTER STUDIES

Character studies are preaching on a person in the Bible, like Abraham, Joseph, David or Peter.

BENEFITS AND DANGERS OF CHARACTER STUDIES

Character studies are beneficial for many reasons. Firstly, Bible characters are interesting, with many failures and sins as well as triumphs! We are warned by the dangers that other men and women of faith faced, as well as strengthened as we learn how their faith overcame times of testing and difficulty. Christians are happy to hear about Bible characters. These studies are neither too academic and dry, nor are they impractical. Because they are personal studies, people connect with them. A second benefit is that we get to preach through books of the Bible that we might otherwise ignore or leave aside as impractical for preaching on – Genesis, Exodus, 1 Samuel, etc. Someone has said that the topical preacher soon wears himself out, while the textual preacher wears his hearers out. Character studies provide variety. We should be preaching on the whole canon of Scripture, including the OT. Character studies give us another way of getting God's Word into hearers' lives and doing them spiritual good. A. P. Gibbs lists three advantages of such studies: (1) Information: human nature is perhaps the most fascinating of all studies, (2) Inspiration: The study of the life of a man of God is, in itself, a spiritual stimulus, awakening and developing a desire for greater godliness of life, (3) Imitation: it should lead to a desire to follow the example of this godly person. There are very few dangers with character studies. One danger is either doing a poor job of a character study or doing too many character studies, which defeats the purpose of providing variety. Another danger is allowing the character to obscure or overshadow the person of Christ in our preaching – although this is very difficult, because most characters have obvious flaws. We want to try and bring out the glories of Christ in our preaching, and the principles of faith in God.

HOW TO DO CHARACTER STUDIES

There are two sorts of characters studies.

1. Firstly, there are the major characters of the Bible: Abraham, Joseph, Moses, David, Peter and Paul – characters which have more than two or three chapters devoted to them. Here, we simply have normal expository preaching in disguise – taking a chapter per message over a period of maybe 8 weeks. We can tell people we are doing a character study, but what we are really doing is simply teaching through a part of a book of the Bible. The normal features of preaching apply: we need to look out for the Main Lesson, or Big Idea from the passage we preach on, we need a clear structure that divides up the passage or lesson, and we need to illustrate and apply it.
2. Minor characters are different. These are cases where we have scattered references to the character over a larger section of Scripture. Here we are not looking for the Big Idea of a particular passage of Scripture, but the main character trait or lesson from the life of this person.
    - <u>Examples</u>: Caleb (means 'dog') – one of the 12 spies, he wholly followed the Lord
    - <u>Examples</u>: Barnabus (means 'son of encouragement'), always encouraging other people

STEPS TO TAKE IN PREPARATION:

1. Read all that the Bible has to say about the person, and dig into the details of their life.
2. List all the main events, and chief character features of this person – good and bad
3. Try to discover the cause or secret of his/her greatness or weakness, and trace the results or consequences that follow from this (i.e. look for Cause and Effect in this person's life)
4. Look out for the main characteristic or chief lesson we learn from the character
5. Get a sermon outline by the main events/incidents, or stages of their career, or lessons we learn.

29 GOSPEL PREACHING

The main difference between evangelistic preaching and other sorts of preaching is not in the form or shape that the sermon takes, but rather in the way in which it is preached. While a gospel sermon should still have an introduction, a main idea, a clear structure, illustrations, applications and a conclusion, the thing that is altogether essential to a gospel sermon is its spiritual power.

THE MAIN SPIRITUAL DIFFERENCE

Richard Baxter the great Puritan preacher said that we must preach 'as one that ne'er should preach again, and as a dying man to dying men'. Because we are preaching to people who might never have heard the gospel before and may never hear it again, a great responsibility lies upon us. The responsibility of preaching the gospel calls for spiritual power that is not our own. Paul could say to the Corinthians, 'When I came to you, I did not come with excellence of speech or of wisdom, declaring to you the testimony of God ... my speech and my preaching were not with persuasive words of human wisdom, but in demonstration of the Spirit and of power' (1 Cor. 2:1, 4). In 1 Thess. 1:5, he wrote, 'Our gospel did not come to you in word only, but also in power, and in the Holy Spirit'.

The great need, therefore, in gospel preaching is spiritual power. This is not to say that we should spend all our preparation time in prayer alone. Paul could write in 2 Tim. 1:7 that 'God has not given us a spirit of fear, but of power and of love and of a sound mind'. Notice: the Holy Spirit helps us to speak in a way that is sensible and clear, as well as powerful. There must still be the three essentials of preaching: truth, clarity and passion (Campbell-Morgan).

Notice how Paul spoke of 'declaring the testimony of God' (1 Cor. 2:1). We have a solemn testimony, a witness to bear. Sometimes we are tempted to skip the more difficult parts of the gospel message, like sin, death and judgment, to avoid offending unbelievers. George Muller said that he saw more results in conversion when he addressed his congregation as 'sinners' directly. Whether this was the secret of his evangelistic success, he definitely did not try to dodge an important part of the gospel proclamation.

OTHER PRACTICAL DIFFERENCES IN A GOSPEL SERMON

1. <u>Shorter messages</u>: unbelievers have less patience with long-winded preachers. We ought to say what we need to say without padding it out or trying to go on too long needlessly.
2. <u>Starting point</u>: the apostles always seemed to start their messages where unbelievers were at, whether it was Paul preaching on idolatry at Athens or Peter using the leaping lame man as a launch point.
3. <u>Simpler</u>: remember the needs of the audience: don't speak about side-issues (unnecessary context), or things they don't know about biblically; try to use more illustrations and avoid religious jargon.

OTHER ISSUES AND QUESTIONS

One question that is often brought up today is whether we should be preaching Christ in every sermon. This is considered not only theologically vital, but evangelistically important. But calls for this usually come from evangelicals who have a 'mixed multitude' of Christians and unbelievers in their churches. Even in their teaching, they want to invite people to trust Christ – fair enough. However, the theological rationale for preaching Christ is sometimes dubious. For example, if you are preaching through certain parts of the Old Testament (e.g. Elijah's ministry), trying to find (or force) Christ into every passage is unwarranted, or at least difficult. It is perhaps better to preach the gospel to unbelievers from clear NT gospel passages, rather than trying to bring Christ out of obscure passages. Better, too, to have a clear inside/outside line between the church (true believers) and those not saved.

30 PREACHING ON NARRATIVES

Preaching on biblical narratives requires a different approach to the way we preach on epistles, prophecies or discourses (speeches). Whereas epistles, prophecies and discourses are logical, narratives have a storyline. If we try to preach an analytical sermon that dissects a story, we will kill it; our message will be as dry and boring as an English literature essay. Instead, preaching on narratives requires us to bring the story to life, so that listeners are drawn into it, feel its power and learn its lessons too. Narratives are mainly found in the OT historical books and in the gospels and Acts. They make up 44% of the Bible – and these are the most interesting parts of the Bible too. Christ taught using parables – memorable stories that convey powerful lessons.

How do stories work? Stories work on **emotion**. Stories involve the introduction of tension or conflict – a problem that needs to be resolved. Then, instead of things getting better, they get worse (the tension is increased). Eventually, there is a resolution and (hopefully) there is a happy ending. Stories also involve Association (and its opposite, Dissociation). That is, we instinctively take sides with the person in need, or the person who has been wronged. We feel their injustices and disappointments and want to see them win. The bigger the problems, the longer we listen to the story, hoping that they win. In the Bible, most stories have these elements of tension, conflict and problems (Joseph sold into slavery, David facing a giant, Jonah disobeying, Jairus desperately hoping Jesus comes in time to heal his daughter). Most Bible stories involve an element of people needing to be rescued from some problem (after all, the Bible is the story of salvation).

How to Preach on Narratives

1. You have to **Tell** the Story. You might think that everybody in your audience has already heard the Bible story you are preaching on, and don't need to hear it again. You think that just reading the Bible passage out will be sufficient. Then you proceed straight to lessons we learn from it. This is a **BIG mistake**. You need to re-tell the story, because this is how stories work – by being told. Be a story-teller.

2. You need to let people **Feel** the story. As we tell Bible stories, we need to help our listeners feel the tension. We do this by helping them put themselves into the same shoes, or situation, as someone in the story (association). Listeners use their imagination to think how they would react in the same circumstances. We can help them do this by saying something like, 'Imagine if you were in this situation ...', maybe even by using a modern-day parallel situation.
3. You need to **Teach the Message** of the Story. You are not just here to tell a story – you also have to preach its message clearly. In other words, look for the 'Big Idea'. Often, biblical stories are all about salvation (the Big Idea of the whole Bible). But sometimes the lesson is something else.
4. You need to **Break Up** the Story. You need to tell the story in 'episodes', or chunks – the main 'scenes'. These will often correspond to the paragraph divisions in modern Bibles. These sections will form the 'Clear Structure' of your message. You need to bring out the individual truths or lessons that the different 'scenes' in the story present. As you re-tell the story, intersperse the individual spiritual lessons we learn in between the storytelling 'scenes'. If you do not have a 'clear structure', preaching on narratives can resemble one long ramble, instead of an exciting story.
5. You need to **Illustrate and Apply** the lessons of the Story. The spiritual lessons you draw from the story (sin, judgment, repentance, faith, grace) are not familiar subjects to all people. They need to be explained or proven by illustrations, and applied to our situation.

Conclude your message. Bring out the Big Idea you have been building, and repeat the individual lessons that together make up the Big Idea. Repeat the story's application with a Call to Action.

31 PREACHING ON POETRY

One third of the Bible is poetry. This not only includes the psalms, but also many of the prophets. There are a few special things about poetry that we need to be aware of in our preaching.

One difference with poetry is that it uses more figures of speech than other types of literature. Thus, the fact that Psalm 91:4 says that God 'will cover you with his feathers' does not mean that God is a bird, any more than verses which say that God is our Rock (Psalm 18:2) mean that He is made of minerals. In the same way, Psalm 34:15 ('the eyes of the LORD are on the righteous, and His ears are open to their cry') does not teach us that God has a physical body, including eyes and ears, although God is like us, having the ability to hear and see. Poetry regularly uses metaphors like these to teach important truths in a more picturesque way. Psalm 19 verses 4-6 do not prove that the earth is flat, or that the sun circles the earth, for it is not making a scientific observation about the sun at all – it is poetic imagery.

PREACHING POETRY

The normal principles for preaching apply to speaking on poetical parts of the Bible. Your preaching must be biblically-faithful, spiritually powerful; it must have one main idea, clear structure, introductions, illustrations, applications and conclusions.

It is in the area of the structure of your message that you will perhaps need to take a little more care when preaching on poetry. This is because there tend to be two types of psalms.

1. Firstly, there are smaller psalms which you will usually be able to split up into natural divisions and use these as your structure. For example, in Psalm 113, there are three stanzas, each of three verses:

   - Praise the Lord (verses 1-3)
   - God is on high yet looks upon the lowly (verses 4-6)
   - God raises the humble and seats them with princes (verses 7-9)

2. Secondly there are longer psalms which have too many divisions to deal with in a simple, memorable structure. Thus, some psalms are acrostics where each verse starts with a letter of the Hebrew alphabet, and these psalms tend to not have neat divisions, but instead deal with similar thoughts on the main theme, like 'pearls on a string'. This is especially true of Psalm 119 (176 verses long), whose main theme is the Word of God. Other long psalms can be repetitive (like some modern Christian songs!), coming back to thoughts that were expressed earlier in the psalm. Therefore, it is usually better to look for important themes threaded though the psalm, and use an almost topical approach to preaching on these psalms. For example, Psalm 18 (50 verses long), seems to deal with one main theme: God's salvation, but it has four sub-themes:

- David calling upon God for salvation
- God's powerful deliverance
- David's innocence
- Praise God!

32 SMALL GROUP STUDIES

Small group Bible studies are different to preaching in that, rather than one person preaching the whole time, other people in the group also contribute comments and questions. However, the same important principles of preaching God's Word also apply to leading a small group Bible study.

SMALL GROUP DYNAMICS

Small groups have their own special dynamics because of the multiple personalities interacting. One sociologist has described the dynamics of a small group using the phrase 'Forming, Storming, Norming, Performing'. 'Forming' refers to the start of a group – this beginning stage is usually polite and generally positive. The 'storming' stage occurs when people's personalities or opinions start to clash with others, resulting in disagreement or friction. A group comes to the 'norming' stage when people get used to each other and appreciate one another's strengths. At the 'performing' stage they work together productively.

Leading a small group Bible study involves steering clear of two extremes. On the one hand, some leaders give a monologue (sometimes because others do not know enough about the Bible) while at the other extreme, there is lots of exploratory discussion but no conclusions reached (a 'pooling of ignorance'). The best small group leaders encourage participation, but also lead the group through a passage to the right answers and lessons. If a small group is evangelistic, there is much more room for people to say 'wrong' things – the key objective there is to let them hear the gospel without clobbering them when they say something wrong. But for Christian Bible studies, truth as well as love are important; we want people to be built up in their faith through properly understanding Scripture.

PREPARING FOR AND RUNNING SMALL GROUP BIBLE STUDIES

The more preparation you put into leading a small group Bible study the more everyone will get out of it (don't go in empty-headed): read the passage, pray over it, makes notes on it (summarise, paraphrase, question it), read commentaries (if you need), think about applications, etc.. Two of the most important features of normal preaching (The Big Idea and Clear Structure) are applicable for small group studies. Announce the big idea in your introduction, and then lead them through the structure, one paragraph or division at a time. This prevents getting bogged down. Explain a leading thought in a division and then direct people to a verse or paragraph for discussion, or ask a well-directed question to get things going. E.g., Daniel 6 (Daniel in the lions den) has a simple structure: vs 1-10 (the trap set by enemies), vs 11-17 (the king's attempts to free Daniel), vs 18-23 (Daniel Saved by God), vs 24-28 (the results).

If you are preparing a sheet of questions (or even if you aren't), you can use four types of questions as you proceed down through the natural divisions (clear structure) of your passage:

1. A Conversation Starter: this is a question to get people to open up. It might be a general question about some aspect of the big idea of your passage, and what people think about this topic, or it might be a more light-hearted question to get nervous people to relax and open up.

2. Observation Questions: these are questions that answer 'what': what is this verse/paragraph talking about. These are usually quite obvious and 'on the surface' questions used to get everybody to first base and establish what the verse/passage is dealing with.

3. Interpretation Questions: these questions deal with problems or difficulties in a verse, for example, deciding between two different alternative views. We answer this sort of question by exploring word meanings, or by looking at the context, or thinking about the historical purpose.

4. Application Questions: these are 'how' questions: how do we put this into practice, what difficulties do we face today, etc. People's experience of life often comes into these sorts of questions.

33 SPEAKING TO YOUTH

Speaking to young people usually involves one of two things: either speaking to a large group or doing a small group Bible study. For both of these two approaches there are some tips that are youth-specific.

SPEAKING TO A LARGE YOUTH GROUP

The normal principles for preaching apply to speaking to youth: biblically-faithful, spiritually powerful, one main idea, clear structure, etc. However, particularly when speaking to non-Christian and unchurched youth, there are some special needs:

- Use a more attention-grabbing introduction
- Use more (and lots of) powerful illustrations – inspirational stories, biographies
- Make the gospel clear and simple
- Use powerpoint, particularly simple images rather than lots of text
- Use video clips – don't go on for too long with the clip, however, just make the point
- Give them and opportunity and time to ask questions

RUNNING A SMALL GROUP STUDY

The same principles apply to running a Bible study group for young people as for other older groups, however, some youth-specific tips apply:

- Don't give them handouts to fill in, or pens. They will just doodle, or make a paper plane.
- Don't seat the kids in a way that makes some seats better than others. You will have behaviour issues if some lounge up the back. Getting them to sit in a circle is good for discussion.

The normal features of preaching and running a small group study apply:
- use a good illustration for a conversation starter,
- if the passage is a narrative, make sure to briefly re-tell the story in your introduction.

- Divide the study up into chunks of verses (clear structure) and look at it sequentially
- Use illustrations to explain a point, and look for applications to make it practical
- Conclude by emphasising the main point.

One Bible study format is to get them to read the passage and get everyone to answer three questions:
1. **Favourite verse**: what verse do you like the most?
2. **A Question**: what question do you have about this passage?
3. **Application**: what is one thing this passage is teaching us, or telling us to do?

OTHER YOUTH GROUP ISSUES AND NEEDS

Running a youth group involves more than Bible studies. These kids have social needs, so running games and putting on outings for them are good. Kids have enormous appetites, so put on some supper for them. You also want to get to know these young people individually so that they will be influenced by your life as well as your teaching. Connect with them outside the official youth group times, spend time with them in daily life, and visit their families to try to get to know their parents. They say that one camp is worth a year of youth group. If young people have become Christians disciple them and get them involved in helping to run the youth group program.

SECTION FIVE:

Children's Messages

34 BIBLE STORYTELLING

TELLING BIBLE STORIES

One of the most memorable lessons I learned in children's work happened in a small village in England (called Steeple Bumpstead!) on a cold winter's night. About 20-30 children (many of them little girls) had gathered in a room in a village school for a children's meeting. The leader told the children a story using a picture-book (it wasn't a bible story, but it was a story with a spiritual lesson). As he began to tell the story in a soft voice, many of the little girls were not listening but were instead fidgeting and whispering to each other, but instead of reprimanding them and asking them to pay attention, the storyteller continued as if they were all listening attentively. As he continued to tell the story and turn the pages of the book, the children became increasingly transfixed and all the noise and movement disappeared. When the story finished, the storyteller went back to the beginning of the book and went over the pages at the beginning that the children had not really paid attention to very well.

There are other methods people recommend for teaching children the Bible, however, stories are easily the most powerful. You probably had no difficulty paying attention to the story in the paragraph above. Some people prefer other methods, like getting children to shout out noises and jump about when key words are read out, or acting out the story as you tell it, or firing question after question at children (instead of just telling them the story). However, none of these methods capture their attention or help them to remember the story as well as good storytelling. Most just result in the kids becoming more hyperactive and inattentive. For example, most primary school kids cannot stand up in front of a class and act out a part in a story without fits of giggles (which quickly become contagious), while continually bombarding kids with questions (to

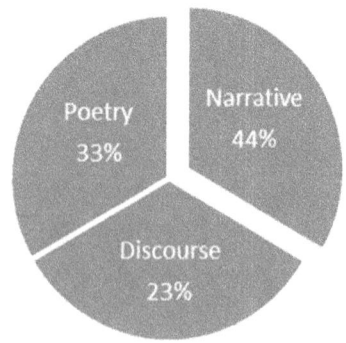

hold their attention) obeys the law of diminishing returns (the more you do it, the less effect it has).

Why become a storyteller?
Because 44% of the Bible consists of narratives – these are the most interesting parts of the Bible for children. Christ taught using parables – powerful (and memorable) stories. We all use stories to communicate to each other – telling about what happened to each other around the dinner table or on the phone. Most modern media involves story-telling: films and TV shows use storylines, and even documentaries and current affair articles deal with issues by introducing us to a person who tells their story.

How do stories work?

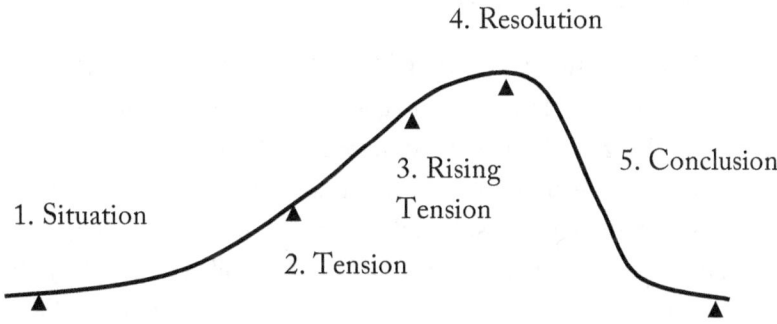

Stories work because of the introduction of tension or conflict – a problem that needs to be resolved. Jane Austen novels do not start with the story of how Emma and Wilfred got married and lived happily ever after. Instead, firstly, Wilfred fails to turn up at the wedding. Then, instead of things getting better (Wilfred turning up late and the wedding proceeding), things get worse (the tension is increased) when Wilfred is found to have been gravely wounded and lingers near death for months (he has been attacked by the wicked Rupert, who proceeds with his money to try to attract Emma to marry him). Eventually, there is a resolution (Emma sees through Rupert and kisses Wilfred, who miraculously recovers) and there is a happy ending.

Stories also involve something called Association (and its opposite, Dissociation). That is, we instinctively take sides with the Wilfreds of the world against the Ruperts. We feel the injustices and disappointments of the Emmas and Wilfreds and want to see them win. The bigger the problems, the longer we listen to the story, hoping that they win.

Similarly, in the Bible, most stories have these elements of tension, conflict and problems (Joseph sold into slavery, David facing a giant, Jonah disobeying, Jairus desperately hoping Jesus comes in time to heal his daughter). Most Bible stories involve an element of people needing to be rescued from some problem (after all, the Bible is the story of salvation). As we tell Bible stories, we need to help our listeners <u>feel</u> the tension by helping them put themselves into the same situation as the character in the story (association). We use our imagination to think how we would react in the same circumstances.

TEACH SPIRITUAL TRUTHS – STORY IS NOT ENOUGH!

Our goal in telling bible stories is to convey God's message to the children, particularly the gospel message contained in the Bible. It is not enough simply to tell a cracking good story (as some Christian storytellers do). These Bible stories contain spiritual truths that need to be brought out for the children. Common Bible truths we find in Bible stories include the fact the fact that we deserve God's judgement for our sins (the OT is full of stories of sinful behaviour), that people need to be rescued from all sorts of predicaments (which finds a spiritual parallel in our need to be saved), that God is the Saviour (not us), that Jesus is God's Son (as seen by the things he did), that Jesus provides the way of salvation through his death and resurrection, and that we need to put faith in God.

Don't leave the lessons to the end. Some children's workers realise that the Bible stories contain important truths, and they realise it is their job to convey these truths, but they leave all the lessons till the end. However, this is not how the TV does things. A story shown on the TV does not run for 45 minutes straight, leaving 15 minutes free at the end for advertisements. If it was, people would switch off at the end of the show and skip the ads. Instead, the ads are spaced throughout the story while the tension remains unresolved and we are left hanging wanting to find out how Wilfred wins in the end. Similarly, the best place to teach spiritual truths in Bible stories is when they crop up, and as evenly spaced as possible. If you tell the story and then spend five minutes at the end teaching some lessons from the story, the children will stop listening as soon as the story finishes.

Normal preaching to adults proceeds by (a) teaching truths derived from the passage, and (b) interspersing these 'heavy truths' with illustrations that hold attention, explain hard things or apply the truths to the lives of the listeners. Speaking to children works exactly the same way, but we reverse the order: the truths are interspersed throughout the storyline, which holds the attention.

USE ILLUSTRATIONS

Illustrations (the sort that preachers normally use) are essential for speaking to children. This is because the spiritual truths we pull out of Bible stories usually involve concepts that most adults find hard to understand, and they are foreign ideas to children too. We need to help children to understand ideas like faith, sacrifice, repentance and grace. So, we need to use illustrations to help them grasp these truths. What we are doing is essentially giving the children yet more stories.

Actually, with children, it is remarkably easy to think of illustrations. You can often come up with an imaginative illustration on the spot by thinking of situations that children face, particularly in the home or school setting. This is because in the home or school setting, there is an awful lot of social interaction among children (they are always getting in trouble, calling each other names, boasting, fighting and making up, disobeying teachers, and displaying all sorts of other sinful behaviours that adults try their best to disguise). This is a reason why children's ministry is so valuable for adult preachers too: it helps preachers with their illustrations. Preachers who never speak to children often use 'canned' illustrations – out of books. They rarely use their imagination, with the result that their imagination withers, and so they are often struggling for decent illustrations.

Where do we get illustrations from?

- from our personal experience,

- from the experience of children – in the school-yard or at home,
- from news and current affairs,
- from our imagination (imagine that there was a girl who …),
- from stories in books or movies that children already know,
- from history,
- from nature,
- from anywhere you can!

Illustrations primarily do three things: (1) explain truths that are hard to understand by relating them to everyday situations, (2) prove truths that people may not be convinced about by using everyday analogies, and (3) apply truths that people need to realise that they must put into action themselves. Of course, illustrations also hold the attention, stick in the memory and perform all sorts of other wonderful services.

Conclusion

The best way of teaching the Bible to children (in my opinion) is

A. Tell them a Bible story,

B. Intersperse the story with Bible truths, and

C. Use illustrations to drive these truths home.

35 PREPARING FOR TEACHING CHILDREN

Some years ago, in teaching Religious Instruction in school, the lesson was on Rehoboam. At the time the syllabus was going through various OT kings and prophets, and there were a number of teachers who were complaining about teaching these stories. Some complained because their children didn't yet know about Jesus, so why bother teaching them about minor and obscure OT personalities? But other teachers were complaining because, I suspect, they did not really have much idea about the lessons that could be learned from these stories.

Most children's workers have no trouble with some Bible stories – it is not very hard to tell the story of the woman who came and touched the hem of Jesus' garment. Nor is it difficult to teach Bible truths from this story (who Jesus is, the importance of faith and the fact that true faith must take action). However, there are other Bible stories that are harder to teach.

Some teachers, of course, feel out of their depth with (certain parts of) the Bible and for their preparation will take a cop-out route and just read the Teaching Manual. Worse, in class they will repeat exactly what the teaching manual says word-for-word straight to the children. This is disgraceful really, because teachers need to be bringing a message from the Lord to the children (a message that has first gripped them), not parroting somebody else's thoughts.

How do we prepare for teaching Bible stories?

A. Continually pray for the Lord's help and guidance in your preparation as you look into His Word

B. Read the story or passage through, preferably in a few different Bible translations

C. Jot down any thoughts or notes as you read (brainstorming). You can also jot down questions of the passage as you read (Why did it say that? What does that mean? How would I feel if I were in that situation? What lesson do we learn from that? etc.). This all helps to get your mind thinking about the passage (i.e. meditating on it). You can also check out the meaning of Bible words in a Bible dictionary that you had trouble with in your reading at this point (if different Bibles use different words or ambiguous language).

D. **Paraphrase** the story, retelling it in your own words. This is probably the single most successful strategy for preparing for children's messages, because (a) when you tell the story, you are in effect paraphrasing it for the children, and (b) putting it into your own words helps you to think more deeply (i.e. meditate) on the passage than any other method - it works your mind hardest.

E. **Summarise** the story, **dividing** it up into its natural divisions. Division is very useful, because when you tell the story, it helps to remember the main 'acts' in the 'play', but summarising is also very helpful because when you try to boil the story down to its essentials, it sometimes reveals the main lessons that the story teaches us (e.g. about faith). It is very important to try to be as focussed as possible in teaching bible lessons to children (i.e. one BIG lesson is easier to remember, for children as well as teachers, than six minor points).

F. Try to identify the main themes or truths that the story teaches as well as trying to identify the main application or lessons that the story leaves us with.

G. Finally, write out your 'message' for the children in **outline** (or note) form, following the basic outline:

   a. Story elements (based on the first DIVISION of the story)
      i. Truths (based on the truths that emerge)
         - Illustrations and applications
   b. Story elements
      i. Truths
         - Illustrations and applications
   c. Story elements
      i. Truths

- Illustrations and applications

What can I skip? Out of all of these preparation steps, there are some that are more important than others, and some which can be skipped. It will probably depend on how familiar you are with the story. If you are really struggling with an unfamiliar passage, the more preparation you do the more you will get to grips with it. Sometimes, the Lord will give you such help that after praying and reading the passage, you can skip straight to G (jotting down an outline of your message). However, this is very rare, and usually, you will want to put down at least a page of preparation notes or paraphrasing. One useful compromise (that I use) is to start paraphrasing the story, and then to turn it into an outline form (that is, a paragraph of story paraphrase, then a 'Bible truth' that emerges, then an illustration (or a space for one), then repeat the process: paraphrase, truth, illustration).

WARNINGS

- Don't stand up the front with your notes. Use your pictures or visual aids (we will come onto visual aids and other similar devices in the last workshop) to help you remember where you are up to in your 'storyline, truths, illustrations'

- Don't just tell the story and tack the lesson on at the end – intersperse these elements.

- **The Main Point**: What happens if you just can't seem to make any headway in your study (no outline, no Bible truths emerging, not sure how it is all going to work out)? We've all been there, so don't worry! Start paraphrasing the story, or start writing down some notes. Don't just sit there staring at a blank page in desperation wondering how it is all going to come together! Act in faith, start 'meditating' by <u>putting pen to paper</u>. Trust God by taking action in faith and <u>it will start coming together</u>!

An Encouragement: Doing your Bible study preparation this way (instead of just re-heating someone else's lesson plan) has an added benefit and bonus: your soul will be blessed and grow. You will get better at teaching children, and very soon others, too.

36 INCREASING YOUR IMPACT

Although teaching the Bible by telling stories is important for communicating the gospel to children, we need to augment the power of storytelling with other means. This is because people do not usually remember very much of what we tell them – only 5%. Instead, if we add visual aids, retention rates go up to 20% (and attention rates increase markedly too). The best way to remember things is by teaching them yourself - 90% (which is why it is a real blessing to be involved in teaching children).

VISUAL AIDS

There are all sorts of visual aids that can aid storytelling. The flannelgraph Bible story types include CEF, Betty Luken, Footsteps of Faith and Pictograph (plus others). You simply need a (black) cloth background to place the pictures on. Even better is to stick magnetic tape (buy from a hardware store) on the back of the pictures and place them on a magnetic board (most classrooms have a magnetic whiteboard, and in other settings I use a smaller whiteboard painted black). The real advantage of magnetic tape, however, is that you can also put up key words for the story next to the pictures (write the words or names of characters on white card) and other illustrative pictures (heaven, heart, boy praying, etc.) to illustrate story and bible truths. Using magnetic tape means that you are not limited to the few visual aids that a particular supplier gives you for the story.

With younger children, you can also let one person put the pictures on the board, and you can let another person hold a special puppet (kangaroo, teddy bear) that monitors the class behaviour.

Powerpoint visual aids are also becoming more available and useful. Here again you can write words on the pictures to emphasise important truths. John Ritchie's Eikon series is very good, and there are others you can find on the internet.

Video clips are also an option (see some resources at max7.org), but have drawbacks. Because the story is usually shown so quickly, there is little time for the kids to think about what is happening. Just as a teacher needs to meditate on the story to unpack its lessons, so the kids need to be able to think about it too. If you leave all the thinking and discussion till the end, the kids quickly switch off. For the same reason, puppets can be effective, but they can also dumb down the message to the point where it is basically about making the Bible entertaining.

Discussion can also be valuable. Of course, the smaller the group the better, because personal contribution levels, the key to learning and retention, increase. However, with children, discussion levels need to be tailored to age. Thus, the younger children are, the less they are able to meaningfully contribute and the more they seek attention or the approval of peers as much as understanding. In other words, discipline is a big problem with younger age kids, but by the later years of primary school, and within clearly defined boundaries, discussion can become valuable. With infants, it is probably better to just tell the story and teach the truths that emerge from it. Also, the more discussion, the less of the story gets told, and you run out of time for other activities which add interest, variety and reinforce the teaching. With older children, discussion can be used as a substitute for the 'bible truth breaks' in the story.

Verbal Learning is another way that you can enhance the impact of Bible stories. Children will learn better if you get them to say certain things. Thus, you can teach them to say memory verses, get them singing, teach them slogans and even use raps (really just poetry dressed up in black).

Worksheets are another great way for kids to learn. They reinforce the lesson that has been taught by writing out the answers themselves. Use them!

Object Lessons are a great way to introduce Bible stories, and the best ones can be found in the Teaching Manuals which will often have some sort of object lesson to start the lesson off before the story begins. This is one of the real advantages of the Teaching Manuals☺.

Quizzes

Probably the most fun way of reinforcing what you are teaching is to have a quiz after the story, in which you retell the story again by asking the kids questions about it. You can do simple quizzes on a whiteboard (noughts and crosses, hangman), or you can adapt common boardgames (snakes and ladders, car races) and make them into A1 size cardboard games, or you can animate powerpoint objects to make the same games. Or, if you want to get the kids really excited, you can do physical skill games, like shooting baskets or darts. The opportunities are unlimited and there are plenty of games already in existence that you can quickly adapt for your situation.

What happens if you forget your visual aids or if the visual aids don't work (e.g. the projector for the powerpoint is not working right)? Use **drama** – get the children to act out the story while you tell it. Or, you can get a child who is a good artist to come and <u>draw</u> the story on the board while you tell it.

ENHANCING LEARNING OR JUST ENTERTAINING CHILDREN?

One of the quandaries of childrens' ministry is the extent to which we are just entertaining children. Some programs seem to rely entirely on entertainment (churches which provide a separate room for children during the service, in which they have computer games, bouncy castles and clowns to amuse them). These entertainment programs get the kids along, but they convey little truth. Other people argue that it is wrong to try to compete with the world and its entertainments, and they simply give dry Bible teaching – without even visual aids.

In justification of visual aids, we see various prophets in the Bible using object lessons to teach Israel about God's purposes (Jeremiah and Ezekiel used this approach), while even Paul admitted that the spiritual level of his audience required that he use 'earthly' illustrations (see Romans 6:19). Christ himself used about 50 illustrations or word-pictures in the Sermon on the Mount.

On the other hand, trying to compete with the world is doomed to fail. If we try to get children to come along to a program by bribing them with prizes or entertainment, they will soon realise that they can get better thrills in the world. Quizzes that offer the excitement of competition can be spiritual counter-productive in that the children only remember the stories to win the quiz, not because of the lessons they teach. Prizes for memory verses or bringing friends can be counter-productive, too, because the prizes need to become better and better to maintain the same attraction. On the other hand, with a Holiday bible club, some parents are probably more impressed by the quality of the craft projects that the children bring home (and the love that goes into the children) than anything else the church puts on for the family – this might result in the family being willing to come along to other things that result in them coming to Christ. Similarly, children who genuinely enjoy such a holiday bible club (because of its entertainment) will continue to want to go along, and might eventually result in the parents coming along to other programs.

The issue of **discipline** is directly related to enjoyment and involvement. If the kids are involved and enjoying what is happening we will have few discipline problems.

SPIRITUAL ISSUES

Ultimately, we have to learn not to put our trust in human devices (visual aids for learning, prizes for coming, entertainment for enthusiasm), and instead put our trust in God to speak through His word to the children.

This means that we have to depend upon **Prayer**, not programs and entertainment. It is only as God's Spirit convicts that God's word is going to impact childrens' lives. We need to realise we are in a spiritual battle – sometimes a class we expect to go really well will go badly and a class that went badly last week will go well this week. We need to be 'watchful in prayer'. Prayer can also be used in another way, that is, if the teacher makes a point of praying in the class, it shows to the children (and class teachers in an RI setting) that you really believe in the things you are teaching and in the God who you are presenting to the children. Similarly, bringing along a **Bible** and showing it to the children, or reading a part of the story from the Bible, shows the children that what we are teaching them comes from the Bible, God's Word – not from our imagination.

While some RI teachers seem to do a pretty dire job of holding the attention of their classes, the fact that they genuinely **love** the children sends a powerful message – their patience, joy and care for the children may be remembered later in life. Likewise, our spiritual effectiveness will be hampered by a **lifestyle** that is not backing up the message we teach, whether it is the case that we are not ourselves really walking with God, day by day, or by other sinful habits.

BIBLIOGRAPHY

Stuart Olyott, *Preaching Pure and Simple*, Bryntirion, 2005
Haddon W. Robinson, *Biblical Preaching*, Baker, 2001
Martyn Lloyd-Jones, *Preaching and Preachers*, Hodder and Stoughton, 1985
Alfred P. Gibbs, *The Preacher and His Preaching*, Walterick, 1964
J. C. Ryle, *Simplicity in Preaching*
Bryan Chapell, *Christ-Centred Preaching*, Baker, 1994
Charles Bridges, *The Christian Ministry*, Banner of Truth, 1967
John MacArthur Jr., *Rediscovering Expository Preaching*, Word, 1992
Jay Adams, *Pulpit Speech*, Presbyterian and Reformed, 1971
Bill Hybels, Stuart Briscoe, Haddon Robinson, *Mastering Contemporary Preaching*, Multnomah, 1989
John R. W. Stott, *I Believe in Preaching*, Hodder and Stoughton, 1982
Donald Miller, *The Way to Biblical Preaching*, Abingdon, 1957

OTHER BOOKS BY THE SAME AUTHOR

Matthew's Messiah: a Guide to Matthew's Gospel

The Most Amazing Prophecy in the Bible: Daniel's Prophecy of the Seventy Sevens

Is the Bible Really the Word of God? The Doctrine of Scripture

Why there Really is a God and What You Need to Know about Him

The End of the World: What the Bible says about the Future

Do Not Quench the Spirit: a Biblical and Practical Guide to Participatory Church Gatherings

Believers Bible Doctrine Handbook: Eighty Christian Truths

Assembly Autopsy: Why Brethren Churches are Dying and How to Revive Them

www.ingramcontent.com/pod-product-compliance
Lightning Source LLC
Chambersburg PA
CBHW070435010526
44118CB00014B/2047